SWILL 2013

Neil Williams

Vile Fen Press

a division of Klatha Entertainment an Uldune Media company

Library and Archives Canada Cataloguing in Publication

Williams, Neil, 1958-
(Jamieson-Williams, Neil, 1958-)

SWILL 2013 / Neil Williams.

ISBN 978-1-894602-32-7
    1. Science fiction--History and criticism.

2. Science fiction fans. I. Title.

PN3433.5.J36 2012   809.3'8762   C2012-901693-4

Previously published as SWILL: 2012
Copyright © 2013
Neil Jamieson-Williams
ISBN 978-1-894602-26-6
PN3433.5.J36 2012   809.3'8762   C2012-901693-4

Published by Vile Fen Press
an imprint of Uldune Media
504 – 635 Canterbury Street,
Woodstock, ON, Canada, L4S 8X9.
www.uldunemedia.ca

Table of Contents

Introducing SWILL 2013

The cover is based on the cover of Sirius Science
Fiction from back in 1975. This was a magazine of
original creation amateur fiction (with one bad fanfic
Star Trek parody). Sirius had only two issues before it
folded - it cost more to publish than it made.

The 2013 SWILLs continued the series on "The Taboos of
Science Fiction" in the column Flogging A Dead Trekie.

With hope, you enjoy SWILL 2013

Neil Williams
August 2024

TRIGGER WARNING

SWILL is written to BE OFFENSIVE. Really, this is one of the premeditated intents of SWILL. It was written to offend back forty years ago and also just twelve years back in time.

It was not written for the sensibilities of those people under 30 years of age in the mid 2020s.

If you are the type of person who becomes so very much traumatised, that you have to curl up into a ball in bed for a week, after watching an episode of Friends where Chandler Bing talks about his father. If you thus find the 1990s sitcom Friends too racist, sexist, homophobic, and transphobic to watch, and you believe in the core of your heart, that this television series should never, ever, be permitted to air again and that all of the recordings and mastertapes of the series MUST be destroyed so there is now no danger that you will ever encounter this television show ever in the future; then SWILL is definitely not for you.

SWILL is offensive to many. That is one of the main purposes of SWILL. Read at your own risk.

You have been warned.

SwILL

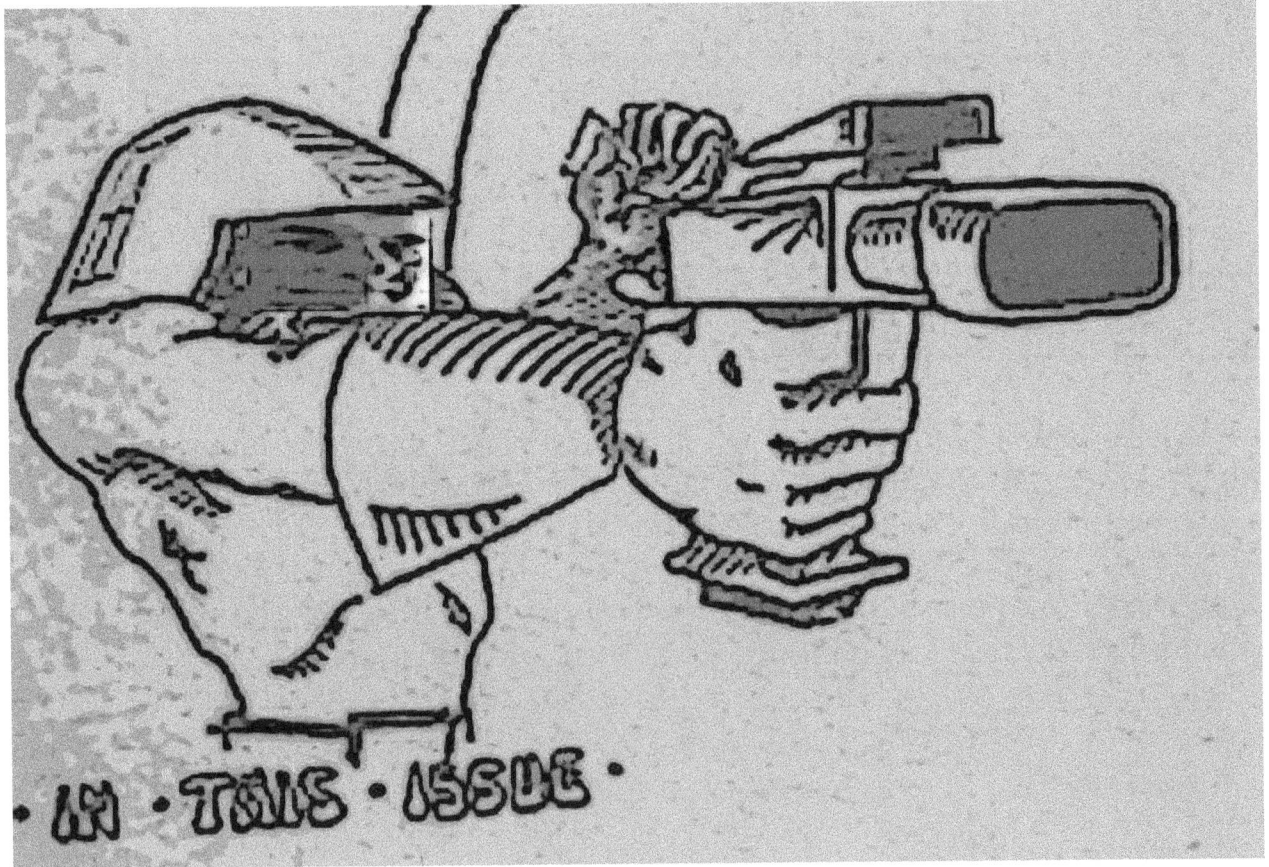

· IN · THIS · ISSUE ·

#18   Spring -- 2013

Table of Contents

Front cover art by Rob Murray and Barb Winkler 1975 for Sirius #1; modified by the editor. Back cover photo taken in 1979/1980 by unknown and originally published in Miriad 2; modified by the editor.

SWILL is published quarterly (Spring, Summer, Autumn, and Winter) along with an annual every February - in other words, five times per year.

SWILL

Issue #18 Spring 2013

Copyright © 1981 - 2013 VileFen Press

a division of Klatha Entertainment an Uldune Media company

swill.uldunemedia.ca

Editorial: Well, Here We All Are...

James William Neilson

So, I'm late again -- the spring issue is coming out in late summer. As things are, I am currently overcommitted with many, many things. In this frenzy of activity, SWILL has had to be shifted to the back burner. For those who are interested, these are some of the things that I have been up to...

Getting a Quebec Birth Certificate:

I was born in Quebec. Up until the late 1970's all I needed was my baptismal certificate, then I required and got an official birth certificate. Sometime in the late 1990's the Government of Quebec, concerned that Quebec birth certificates were easy to forge (they were more difficult to forge than those of the Province of Ontario), decreed that all birth certificates issued prior to X date had expired. I didn't realise this until years later when you now required a passport to travel to the United States and I discovered that my birth certificate was no longer valid. Obtaining a new one wasn't easy as the Government of Quebec had made it difficult for non-residents of the province. They have relaxed the regulations recently and I have just finished jumping through all the required hoops and I should receive a new Quebec birth certificate in a couple of weeks so that I can now get a Canadian passport. BTW, this has been the brief version of this story.

Work:

Re-writing my major textbook. Originally this was to be just an update, but enough things are changing with technology (increased surveillance systems, 3D printing, etc.) that the last four chapters required a fully re-write. On top of that I am also adding in more pedagogical tools (i.e. more charts, graphics, boxes, glossaries, and study aids) to the new text; the manuscript is due to the publisher for early November.

Prepping courses for the coming year. This may seem simple, but you do have to really update videos, etc. as today's students consider any video over three years old as obsolete and so on. In addition, in our modern internet age, one has to come up with new assignments to combat academic dishonesty (there are a few things that I don't like about Turnitin, so I don't use it).

Electronic learning is also taking up a lot of my time, most of which I am doing on my vacation time and weekends.

- Reason One, I don't have sufficient time to do this work when I am teaching.
- Reason Two, it takes far more time to develop this material than claimed by my employer's formula of 3 hours development time (research, writing, recording, post-production, and editing) for every hour of online content.
- Reason Three, if I do this work at work, my employer owns it outright (community college profesors in Ontario have no intellectual property rights).

Add to that the fact that the approach of my employer, The Council (of Community Colleges), and the Ministry (of Training, Colleges, and Universities) to electronic learning is pedagogically unsound, but you have to do what you are ordered to anyway. In brief, this trio wants community college faculty to alter courses to improve student retention and student success (that means to "dumb it down" so that more students pass and graduate). So it takes more time to do the minimum of what you are required to do while still retaining course integrity and quality.

Writing:

To date, I have written six short stories (two so far for my experiment in SWILL) averaging 3,500 words per tale. I have also been re-writing Only Fools and Knaves as a complete novel and that project is on track for its planned November release date. I am also writing an academic work that should be out in around the same time. Finally, I am working on a television script (not a top priority project). For major projects, I work best when I have multiple, very diverse projects on the go; when the muse leaves me or I block or stall on one, I shift over to one of the others. It seems to work for me...

Political Activism:

I am involved in a local political group whose goal is to de-amalgamate the Town of Dundas from the City of Hamilton -- Dundas and other towns surrounding Hamilton were forcibly amalgamated into Hamilton, against the will of these municipalities, by the Province of Ontario twelve years ago. The province is about to merge ward boundaries so that Dundas no longer has its own ward and any real voice on city council.

Research:

Transcribing fieldnotes, coding notes, etc. Finalising the Survey (oh, that early one was just an exploratory survey) for release this Fall. Literature searches and reading any new sources I encounter and making notes.

Nevertheless, I will endeavour to have the summer issue of SWILL out before it is actually autumn.

Thrashing Trufen: Engines Victorious

James William Neilson

Over the past couple of years I have noticed a familiar panel
topic at the conventions I have attended. This topic is usually
phrased as: where has the hopeful future gone, why is the future
darker, etc. In brief, where did the Trek-like better world for
all, onward and upward with technology, all problems solvable,
disappear to? I am going to be nice, sort of, and not even
question how wonderful these happy happy futures really were
(even Trek-land) and just answer the question as honestly as I
can...

Realism happened.

There was a time, when I was young, that I didn't accept the
notion of the corporate state or of corporate hegemony in science
fiction as being realistic. Usually this occurred after some
sort of plague, very limited nuclear war, famine, etc. that
caused all of the governments of the major and middle powers to
fail and thus the multinational corporations stepped in to fill
the vacuum. I didn't buy into this scenario then. I couldn't
see all the major powers of the world failing and I certainly
didn't find it plausible that, should the government of the
Soviet Union or the People's Republic of China collapse, that it
would be replaced by a corporate state. A military dictatorship,
that was plausible, but not a takeover by capitalist
corporations. I liked the innovation in the cyberpunk sub-genre,
the low grade rebellion of the cyberspace hackers, but didn't
accept the emergence of corporate hegemony. The governments
wouldn't allow it... That's not going to play in the Soviet
Union or China... These were simply cautionary tales of futures
to be avoided.

Well, those futures are on the rise.

Actually, there were potential trends in our society back thirty
or forty years ago towards these futures; if you noticed them
(and no, I didn't notice them back then). Corporate tax used to
provide the Government of Canada with close to 30 percent of its
revenue as did personal income taxes fifty years ago; today

corporate tax accounts for 13% and personal income taxes 50% of the government's total revenue. But, this shift is not new; it had already presented itself in the 1970s - it has just become more favourable for the corporations since then. If you are in the middle class, your standard of living has declined. Compensation (salaries/wages) have progressed at below the rate of inflation, there are more users fees, more privatisation of government services, your federal tax has gone down slightly, but your provincial and municipal taxes have risen. You are worse than a mouse on an exercise wheel, running but not just going nowhere, you are falling behind. All of our new technology that was supposed to bring us more leisure time at the same rate of compensation - a shorter work week with no loss in pay - has brought the opposite; massive layoffs, downsizing, and longer hours worked (it has brought substantial cost savings and profits for the corporate powers). The slow erosion of democracy, [1] the increased surveillance of the populace, and so on (I could continue this list, but I shall move on)...

The thing is, there has been no seizure of power by the corporate transnationals from our elected governments; governments have been slowly, increment by increment, permitting their power to be eroded away to the corporations and at an accelerated pace since the fall of the Soviet Union and the collapse of state socialism. And in this new world, creating a better world for all is not on the agenda. Onward and upward through technology is no longer viewed as the secular salvation that it used to be. New technology doesn't necessarily result in an improvement for society, in the short term and in the long term, though it usually does bring us short term advantages. Are all problems solvable? We are less confident that that is possible and any solutions we are certain will have consequences; there will be new problems. And at the root, the foundation, is the central problem of all modern economic systems (capitalist, mixed, or socialist) that is viewed as an externality and thus ignored; that economic theory claims that it is possible to have infinite growth within a closed system.

If you realistically look at the near future -- the next fifty years -- it looks grim. We will have new technology, but there

---

[1] One thing about most American SF, and most American political thought; corporations are not pro-democracy. They are only pro-democracy when there is an alternative that has wide support like social democracy and state socialism. Otherwise, corporations hate democracy and they are NOT democratic organisations. It has been said that when you step through the door into your place of work, you have entered into a fascist organisation.

is no guarantee that there will be access to all citizens or to all people on the planet -- but our elites will get the benefits. Feudalism -- the notion that some people (of noble birth) were more fit to rule based on heredity -- lasted in one form or another for a few thousand years and was based upon unsubstantiated claims backed up by force of arms. What about a near future where our elites have genetically engineered their children (and maybe even themselves), enhanced themselves with nanotechnology and advanced cybernetics, so that they are actually superior to use unaugmented lumpen prol members of Homo sapiens sapiens? Will they want that power shared with the rest of us? No. If they can, via these enhancements, survive in the cesspit that they have made of the world, will they save the rest of us? No. These technologies are being researched, they will (in time) be developed, they will be expensive, and they will not be available to the average person.

There are solid reasons why the future looks darker today than it did in the past, that's because it is darker.

Pissing on a Pile of Old Amazings:

...a modest column by Lester Rainsford

The vagaries of the production schedule of a Multiple Award
Willing publication ~~such~~ whikch is Swill means you could be
reading this in midsummer sipping chablis under a leavy tree.
However as this is written, there is snow. Lots of it. "Up the
wazoo" being the technical term. ~~Also~~ Besides which,it is cold,
and not warm neither. Which brings us to one of Lester's first
disillusions about science fiction, which is that it's always
worth reading.

Actually in this case it was fantasy, a series which was popular
and controversial way back when, the Thomas Covenant series by
Donaldson. The controvery was about a rape scene, which Lester
found neither controvsioal nor discontroversial. What amazed
Lester was a bit where Covenant plops into the 'land' and has to
walk sixty miles. In fresh snow, 'cause it's cold. This was, to
Lester, rather amazing, and he kept reading hoping to find out
what the sectrit superpower of Covenant might be. You see,
Covenant ~~is a leper~~ has leprosy: "damnit Jim I'm a leper not a
protagonist" is his repeated whine. Lepers have poor circulation.
To walk sizty miles in the snow is pretty amazoing. Oh yes,
Covenant was barefoot. Ha! Must have superpowers!

However, as Leter plodded on (a slow reader, he is), there was no
indication of any superpowers. ~~the series~~ The writing was slow,
so that Lester started reading every other page and found that he
wasn't missing out on any plot or description. Just before he
gave up entirely, he was reading the first and last pages of each
chapter only, and theat was sufficient to see that the weries was
afflicted by the 'California syndrome" as Lester would put it.

The Californai syndrom is that ~~peop~~ writers do scenes in bad
weather when they are basically clueless about what bad weather
entails. "I successfolly drove myu car through the miserable
fifty-degree [F of course, these are Californians] to the shoe

store five miles away [two exits of the freeway] therefore my
character must be able to walk sixty miles in the snow barefoot,
that's hardly any more exertion. They think. Add to that the
logical need to make your Token Quest (i.e. quest for multiple
Plot Tokens) more ipressive than the other California writers'
Token Questes, and pretty soon you have paraplegic cystic
fi9brosis sufferers, whoa are additionally in the last stages of
bone cancer, making their way around a planet waist deep in
liquid nitrogen. Uphill both ways.

Human beings <u>are</u> capable of some pretty amazing feats--read about
the "Winter Journey" that Scott's expedition did (and these guys
lived). The went for a multi-week plod over the Antarctivc in
winter, which is to say when it's black night and the temperature
can bi sixty below(F). And yes they suffered and yes they
survived. There is no idnication that any of them were lepers,
though.

So when you the writer has the hero sitting on his horse,
travelling for days in the rain because this is the plot point
where the Evil Forces of the North (evil always comes from the
north, there must be something in the water in Iqaluit) look like
they are about to win, well here's what you do. Go to your local
thrift second hand store, get a ratty woolen blanket. Wear a
ratty wool sweater and wooklpants, cotton os <u>not</u> recommended. So,
now sit on a park bench through a rainy day. No food, no trip to
Timmies for a cruller and a double double, just sit on the park
bench. Lester does not know horses, but it's pretty reasonable to
assume that being on horseback in the wet cold rain is going to
be if anything worse than being on a park bench in the wet cold
arain. (Unlike your '94 Camry, horses don't have roofs, or a
defroster. And no place to plug in your ipod.) Okay, you lasteed
a day, so now sleep under the bench with whatever food you may
have been able to scrounge up (raw swquirrel or pigeon is
likely). And repeat sitting on the bench the next day.

At this poitn, you can either say, 'yes, this is delightful, I am
ready to take on All Evil in the World', which is what your hero
has to do after this cold miserable journey, or you can say,
'gee, my hero has died of exposure' and figure out how to fill
<u>that</u> plot hole.

Lester's decidedly nonscientific theory is that progress was so
limited in the past, and historical figures did really odd and
inexplicable things, because they were exhausted and muddled by
an existence where there was no central heating nor freezers full
of tasty microwaveable dinners nor mechanical contrivances that
can whistk you across town, province, or country in a matter of
hours or days in complete comfort except when the restrooms
havne't been cleaned recently. Therefore, if you r fantasy (or
science fiction) character has some teremendous journey or to
makie, against vast odds, at the end of it your protag will need
a long rest and recovery; your protag will not go on to develop
relativity and ninja-slow-motion swordfight the evil legions into
the ground. When you're tired and cold and hungry and wet and
dirty all the time, Advancing the Cause of Humanity and
Vanquishing the Ancient Evils is a pretty low proiority in your
mind.

Maybe Califorinia writers should model their Quests on the
experience of finding a parking spot at the mall on Black Friday.
There would be some realism at last.

By the way, Lester never did finish the first Covenant series,
never mind the rest. He does wich that the lesson of "you don't
have to finish reading this tripe" hasd been learned when he
tackled the Sword of Shannara, a book which he read in its
entirety despite realising by at least the halfway point that
this was one of the worst books ever written. (Lester was
unfamiliar with the trends in Peirs Anthony's work, and for the
most part is mercifully ignorant of this and late Heinlein as
well. So Shannara as a first hand experience was indeed one of
the worst books ever written.)

So here's the chanllenge: an action series describing the
travails of our hero who can't even find parking close to the
most obsucure mall entrance, and then has to find and ~~rpeire~~
procure This Season's most Sought After Toy. Please keep it under
~~three~~ ~~five~~ seven volumes, and for god's sake don't die before
finishing. Thanks, and reserve a space on your shelf ofr the
inevitable Hugo!

Flogging a Dead Trekkie:

Violating the ~~Taboos~~ Norms of Science Fiction

Part 2 of 8 – Dystopian Despair

James William Neilsen

Malzberg's Taboos of Science Fiction or in my terminology, Norm Violations. These are story concepts and/or plots that if written -- if the norms are violated -- are unpublishable; no professional editor in the genre will touch these stories with a three-metre pole, and certainly would never, ever publish them.

NORM VIOLATION ONE: Dystopian Despair

"Bleak, dystopian, depressing material which implies that the present cultural fix is insane or transient and will self-destruct . . . that the very ethos and materials of the society...will bring it down."

Yuck; who wants to read that shit? Dark, bleak, hopeless tales that focus on society undertaking slow-motion suicide via a melange one litre of head-in-the-sand ignoring of problems, 500 grams of apathy, and 250 ml of no concern for the future as it travels along the road to self destruction. It provides an unpleasant answer to the question of the meaning of life -- either that it is pointless and without merit, or simply without meaning, period.

Now, I read a fair bit of this sort of story back in the seventies when New Wave was still an active sub-genre in SF. Of course, for most of that decade I was in my teens and adolescent angst tends to attract to this type of dark and moody style of fiction. And, for the younger readers, not all New Wave was about Dystopian Despair. Also, there was a larger cultural trend going on during that decade the golden age of the disaster film, which also included post-apocalyptic plotlines. That meant that SF writers, even those with no connexion to New Wave, joined in the carnival of disaster and despair. But there is a major departure between disaster/post-apocalyptic fiction and society engaged in self destruction fiction; in the former, the cause can be external and out of human hands, while for the later, it is always our own fault.[2]

The whole style of story, the bleak tale of societal self destruction, has merit. It can be cautionary and serve as a warning or wake-up call, at very least it can serve to illustrate just how fragile civilisation is and just how dependant we are upon our technology. Nevertheless, I do not recommend a steady diet of this type of SF because, it IS depressing. At the same time, there should always be some of it present, just as a reminder.

Because, guess what; we have problems, lots of them. And they are all nastily complex, interwoven, real, and deadly (to civilisation if not to the species as a whole) with no simple, easy solution at hand.[3] To solve these problems (and we're going to have to solve them) is going to be difficult, will require sacrifices, will involve economic disruptions, will necessitate co-operation, and will probably require a reduction to or the elimination of nation-state sovereignty in the course of implementation. And this is why we prefer to ignore these problems until such time when it is impossible to do so rationally. Some say, and I agree, that that time has already arrived. However, one has to be a forward-thinking person to have that perspective. Within a global civilisation that defines

---

[2] The former also carries the meme in American SF that all the bad things happen to non-Americans -- the Commies, the Europeans, the Asians, the Africans, the Central and South Americans -- the major damage and death tolls by the hundred million happen elsewhere (sure, Washington, New York, and LA may be destroyed but the rest of the US of A abides). With the subtext that the right people have been culled and that the right people, that is the Americans, have survived and that now the world can be a much better place.
[3] Overpopulation, habitat destruction (including deforestation, soil degradation, overharvesting, and invasive species introduction), pollution, increased inequality, resource depletion, and anthropogenic climate and biosphere change.

long range thinking within the context of a 3 to 5 year business plan or the next quarter, the dominant worldview is that none of these problems are PROBLEMS THAT MUST BE SOLVED, yet. We are still waiting for the CRISIS that makes it a certainty, even to the dense and those most committed to avoiding reality, that this is a crisis and something must be done about it. In the meantime, we are speeding toward tomorrow at 150 kph with the edge of a 200 metre drop straight ahead of us; there is uncertainty regarding how far in the distance that cliff edge is, as well as the quality of our brakes and our steering column, but we're flooring it, regardless.

Why is this type of story a norm violation? Because it raises a real issues. Because it makes us think about the new unthinkables.[4] Because it makes us question; perhaps everything. Because it makes us see responsibility and consequence for our actions. Because it is unsettling and makes the reader uncomfortable.

Far better to give the reader a tale where the rationalistic, damn the red-tape protagonist, through a mix of common sense and the scientific method, identifies the simple solution that had eluded the politicians, bureaucrats, and their experts, and saves the day. But, don't call it science fiction; give it the proper label of fantasy (okay, I'll allow calling it science fantasy).

As for my story? What, you thought I'd print it here; well that would bollocks the experiment... Norm Violation One Story is a slightly satirical dark comedy of our own extinction by our own hand -- sort of, we actually delegate it. This story is currently out for consideration at Market #1 and I will report on its progress next time.

---

[4] The old unthinkable was global thermonuclear war -- still a possibility, but it now has company.

Scribbling on the Bog Wall:
Letters of Comment

James William Neilson

As I write this, there is only a single LoC this time around. My comments are, of course, in glorious pudmonkey.

1706-24 Eva Rd.
Etobicoke, ON
M9C 2B2

May 25, 2013

Dear Neil:

I think I got notification on the latest issue of Swill, no. 17, and I checked my records...I didn't know that issue 16 had come out, so here's some comments on both.

16...I would think that by now, even some Americans who would put themselves on the far right of the political spectrum would roll their eyes at some of the purely stupid and ignorant remarks that come out of the mouths of some politicians. Republicans, are you really that dumb? Really? Some Americans are extremely ignorant, some aren't, and some are purely isolated from the realities of the world because they haven't stuck their noses outside of their homes, except to go to church and the bingo hall. The world would be a little saner if the US government didn't have to stick its nose into the affairs of other countries and justify it by saying they are looking out for American interests. I have never understood the need to be armed, unless the whole justification is that one average American is afraid of the next average American, because you never know what they will do. Many Americans must think that the NRA is the greatest curse in American life today, probably on a par with the Tea Party. I could never see myself moving to the USA...I think life there can the capacity to be toxic. Before anyone thinks I am being smug, Canadian aren't far behind their American friends, and a

change in government could help us here a lot. Unfortunately,
both US parties are far right in comparison to any party here.

Hi Lloyd,

Well, I think that I have had enough of a vent on the gun culture of the
USA. It was stupid 30 years ago and is even more stupid today... And I
agree that while our current government would love to allow every
Canadian (or at least every Albertan) to own automatic weapons for
home defence, they also know that the majority of the population
doesn't support this. As for the two major USA parties, the old joke still
holds; the Democrats are akin to the left wing of the Conservative Party
and the Republicans are the same as the right wing of the Conservative
Party.

Pudmonkey is a little rough on the eyes, but it is not
impossible. Hasn't stopped me yet from responding, has it? It
will affect you only if you let it. Just hope you don't find
anything worse. :-) I suspect that the reactions to Pudmonkey is
part of your research, anyway.

Uh, no, it's not. Really, as stated previously, Pudmonkey was selected
back in 2001 for the 20th anniversary Swill Online website for one
reason only -- imperfect memory recall. I didn't have any copies of the
original SWILLs (#1 through #6) and thus selected a font that I thought
mimiced that of the old manual that the Maplecon Slandersheet was
written on. As it turned out, even that old typewritter was cleaner than
Pudmonkey. Most of the original issues -- smudged mimeo aside -- are
more like that of VTCorona. Nevertheless, there is now a tradition to
uphold and so Pudmonkey remains for my LoC comments and for article
titles. In addition, SWILL has won an Elron for the font!

I don't begrudge you your studies of this sometimes-entertaining
subculture we've devoted so much time and effort into...once you
come to some conclusions, I'd like to see them. I can't figure
out this bunch half the time, and I've been here for over 35
years now.

Not quite there yet... Getting close, the Autumn issue should have some conclusions based on the qualitative data collected to date.

Maplecon, that brings back memories. I think I was at that 1981 Maplecon. There are always some people who use their uniforms to terrorize the attendees. I've told a couple of them to fuck off over the years…damned childish cop-wannabees. I haven't done much programming for SFContario, but we acted as guest liaison for Chris Garcia, the FanGoH. This year, we've taken a dealer's table. Might as well try to make a few bucks.

A wee note on Maplecon in the Endnote...

This very morning, I spent some time at this weekend's Anime North helping with next year's CostumeCon 32, to be held in Toronto next year. Too big for me, too crazy, especially in the dealer's room. Polaris in Toronto is gone, and Con*cept is gone in Montréal, but there is also Anime North with an attendance capped at about 20,000, and it looks like the pro-run Wizard World comics convention has abandoned Toronto, so the hard times are being spread around. I think the pros will still win because there is money to be made, and more and more people want to be entertained at fan-run cons instead of doing the entertaining. Passive entertainment is king, and active entertainment is going away…we are basically lazy. Yet…I have noticed that while the pro-run cons are still fairly healthy, fan-run cons are taking on subjects the pro-runs haven't touched. As examples…Burlington and Canadian ToyCons, Art-O-Con (Burlington, big dealer's room), GenreCon (Guelph, nerd culture), Con-G (Guelph, anime), Frostcon (Toronto, nerd culture), and there are other little conventions for specialty toys, furry fandom, comics, anime and gaming. They are all small and growing.

We have both been around for a long time... You have been constantly involved and I have stepped out and gafiated for a couple of decades -- though I still observed a bit on the sidelines (BBSs and later the internet allowed for that). In a way, based on Southern Ontario cons, there would seem to be a bit of the "same as it ever was" going on. I remember in days of yore (late 1970's and early 1980's) that there was a period when there were one or two big Toronto conventions and a whole horde of little ones -- many of which only ran a couple of years. Most of those little cons back then were devoted to mediafen or gaming or both. And most of them were run by younger fans back in the day as gaming and media SF&F were not considered as real SF&F and those who were into that variety of SF&F were not viewed -- by the movers and shakers -- to be real fans. I think the whole "nerd/geek culture" fashion (it's more than a fad but not really a movement) will, in time, become partially absorbed into SF&F fandom as a whole as yet another facet of SF&F fandom. And as that happens, it will eventually have its own big Toronto fan-run convention that also include programming for other niches of fandom.

I would disagree that these younger fans are lazy and into passive entertainment only; they ARE putting on their own conventions and it would appear that active, participatory entertainment/programming is something that they place emphasis on. At present, they also seem to be less to unfannish in the way that you and I view being fannish (and certainly unfannish to fans like Taral). Again, as I have stated before, part of this shift has to do with mediums of communication that are available today which means that new fans of SF&F (and there are a lot of them) are not being socialised into the subculture by the previous generations; they are charting their own paths and developing their own norms and values that, from the viewpoint of older fans, are unfannish.

Con*cept may be gone, but I am pretty certain that a new Montreal convention will emerge. Polaris is gone and time will tell if Reversed Polarity will be its phoenix. Ad Astra continues. Although I don't know the exact reasons, I am pretty certain that Wizard World pulled out of Toronto as it didn't want to battle head-to-head with Fan Expo (and their comic con) on Fan Expo's home turf.

17...Fannishness and unfannishness is in the eye of the beholder or the critic. It's all subjective. At least you got the issue done, and not everyone pubs their ish. When it comes to any book, your mileage may vary, as will its level of shittiness. Why do we tear each other down over our choice of reading materials? With today's dropping literacy levels, we should be please that anyone is reading anything.

Because fans are people (and therefore human) and those who are literary fans are going to judge others by the books that they read. And those who are media fans are going to judge others by the shows that they watch. You find it occurs within other genres too, it's just that SF&F fans are more in contact with one another than say, fans of political thrillers.

Let's see what you write, and how good it is, and how it violates those norms. If you can put these seven stories together, you might just get a writing books out of it. Worth a shot.

Well, for the experiment to work, I will only discuss the premise of the stories written and their progress or lack thereof within the marketplace. As I am going to try and sell them, they won't be appearing in SWILL, unless they have exhausted all of the pro and near-pro markets (e.g. InterZone, On Spec). Even then, I am more likely to collect them and publish them via my imprint. But thank you for the encouragement.

Your comments to Graeme Cameron...I think you fit in as a local observer of fandom, recording all its foibles and warts. I appreciate what you do; I wish more would take notice. The community of fandom identifies themselves as such, having found through some books that the community exists. It took me some years to find that community, and while it was fairly unfriendly at first, others took me in to show me the local ropes.

I was definitely a full-fledged member of the SF&F community when I lived in Vancouver. With the Toronto community, there was no notion of a GTA back then and if you didn't live in the city you really weren't fully a member of that community. Today, I live outside of the GTA and thus remain peripheral to the Toronto community except via the internet.

```
I understand your Endnote...this isn't worth endangering your
employment over.  I quite understand, Jim. However, your employer
has already branded your topic of research as freaks and weirdos,
so have they already passed judgment on your work. Have they
invalidated their own support of your work with this, or can you
still continue on with an objective study? I hope they haven't
hamstrung you and your research.
```

This is not much of a problem as there was no support in the first place. When I started here, the attitude was; if you so desire, you can do research and publish, but don't expect to be rewarded for it like at university. Now, unless we can control your research topic and conclusions, we don't want you to perform research and publish -- though we lack the legal power to stop you from doing so -- and will make it difficult (i.e. throw up barriers) for you should you persist in conducting research and publishing. The only thing that has changed is that now I shall be using a pen name/byline for anything recent (post-March 2013) that I publish.

```
Two issues, and I am caught up again! Hope you're having a good
weekend, and let's see what appears in issue 18.

Yours, Lloyd Penney.
```

Till next time...

Endnote: Random Thoughts

James William Neilson

Graeme's Latest Project

Graeme, in last the last ish, offerred to become a SWILL
columnist. This offer was accepted by the editor.
Unfortunately, for SWILL, another project (in addition to all of
his fanzines, being Secret Master of the Elrons, the Canadian
Fanzine Fanac Awards, etc.) has taken priority -- the Canadian SF
Fanzine Archive.

This online archive has the stated goal of "celebrating
traditional Canadian science fiction 'fannish' fandom" -- the
deconstruction of this 'mission statement' shall be the subject
of a future article. Nevertheless, the archive is an undertaking
that SWILL supports; it can be found on the web, here:

http://www.cdnsfzinearchive.org/

SWILL #3 through #5 found

Thanks to the Canadian Science Fiction Fanzine Archive, scans of
issues 3, 4, and 5 of the original SWILL are now available. Here
is a brief revision of SWILL history based upon the new
information. Issues 1 to 4 published in Ontario (February,
March, April, and May). Issue 4.5 -- perhaps called Worldcon
Special Issue or something like that -- printed in time for the
Worldcon in Denver. This issue would have contained an editorial
arguing that the Worldcon should more correctly be called
Americon and a reprint of "The American Weigh". Don't know what
the cover was, or whether I recycled a previous cover. Issue 5
came out in late September and issue 6 in late November/Early
December. More on this in SWILL #19

The Maplecon Mystery Solved

Okay, SWILL #5 makes it official; I trust my recall of events in 1981 of what happened in 1979 and 1980 much more than I do here in 2013. It would definitely appear that I attended Maplecon 2 in 1979 with the Droogs and Fritz and Maplecon 3 in 1980 with Lester and Andrew. And while all of the Droogs did attend Maplecon 3, we were not in droog costume (the last convention we did the droog group costume at was Worldcon 1980 in Boston).

However, overweight Trekies in Original Series redshirts running through the convention floor with phasers would appear to have been an unofficial feature of both Maplecon 2 and Maplecon 3.

Pith Helmet and Propeller Beanie Tour

The face-to-face participant observation portion of the research project is starting to wind down (PO will continue via the internet, etc.). Here are the final tentative tour dates as they currently stand...

August 2013   Fan Expo -- Toronto (one day)

November 2013   SFContario 4 -- Toronto

April 2014   Ad Astra -- Toronto

August 2014   Loncon 3 -- London, UK

November 2014   Reversed Polarity 2 -- Toronto

November 2014   SFContario 5 -- Toronto

SWILL

· IN · THIS · ISSUE ·

#19   Summer --- 2013

Table of Contents

Front cover art by Rob Murray and Barb Winkler 1975 for Sirius #1; modified by the editor. Back cover photo taken in 1979/1980 by unknown and originally published in Miriad 2; modified by the editor.

SWILL is published quarterly (Spring, Summer, Autumn, and Winter) along with an annual every February - in other words, five times per year.

SWILL

Issue #19   Summer 2013

Copyright © 1981 - 2013 VileFen Press

a division of Klatha Entertainment an Uldune Media company

swill.uldunemedia.ca

Editorial: One More (With Hope Final) Time...

James William Neilson

So, here I am again, much to the annoyance of Taral and the
FanStuff set, with categories for fandom. These categories will
be the working categories for my final survey. Over the past two
years I have taken in a lot of input from various fans, including
Taral (we disagree, but the opinion was considered), and this has
gone into the development of these current categories. So, once
again, without further ado, here they are:

Genre Consumers:

These individuals consume science fiction and fantasy content in
a variety of mediums from print to television to gaming, etc.
They may also have an interest in science fiction and fantasy
collectables. They are the major audience for conventions like
Comic Con or Sci-Fi Fan Expo or Dragon Con and they may, on
occasion, attend large regional fan-run conventions. People
within this group do not identify themselves as SF fans. These
persons would be viewed as "mundanes" by fans; however, while
these people exist outside of the science fiction fan community,
they are strong supporters of the genre. These folks love the
genre (as a whole or within a particular medium) but are either
oblivious of fandom or have no interest in fandom.

Recently, at the conference Science Fiction: An Interdisciplinary
Genre (an English Literature/Cultural Studies conference in
honour of Rob Sawyer donating his archives to the McMaster
Library) I had the opportunity to talk with a number of people
who consumed the genre, enjoyed the genre, wrote professionally
about the genre, but did not consider themselves to be science
fiction fans. As these persons were all academics, they quickly
related the word fan to its origin (in English) of fanatic and
made it abundantly clear that they were not fanatics; still, they
were all genre consumers.

It is from this population that the majority of the people who
make up the science fiction fan community emerged from (while

there are a few cases of individuals discovering fandom first and
then the genre, for the majority, they discover the genre and
then fandom).

Fans:

The central difference between a genre consumer and a fan is that
a fan perceives themself as being a fan -- of the genre, as an
identity, and as a member (in one form or another) of a fan
community. And from that one single commonality that unites all
SF fans, the kaleidoscope emerges. Everyone has their lists and
categories and whatever; there are lumpers and splitters,
inclusive definitions and exclusive definitions, and it is one
big hodgepodge. I am quite willing to leave it at that -- I am
more interested in wider terminology.

Fannish Fans:

Those fans who engage in fan activity that is viewed as
being fannish by other fannish fans and therefore is highly
subjective and mutable geographically and temporally. For
example; when I was a young fan in Ontario, mediafen, even
those who published their own fanzines and organised media-
oriented fan-run conventions, were not considered to be
fannish fans. That has changed over the past thirty odd
years and, of course, those people are considered to be
fannish today. Another example, in Vancouver (around the
same time period), the definition of fannishness was more
inclusive and already, albeit grudgingly, accepted mediafen
of the type mentioned above as being fannish. True, in both
regions at that time, the preferred definition of a fannish
fan was that of the literary SF fannish fan. Thus, who is
and who is not a fannish fan is rooted within regional and
temporal context and those contexts are not locked in
stasis, they change.

What that also means is that the fan activity of today`s
younger fans, largely seen as being unfannish by present
fannish fans, in all probability will be seen as fannish in
time, if the new forms of fan activity persist, as this
style of fan activity is incorporated into the SF fan
subculture. The fact that the under thirty segment of
fandom are organising their own conventions with emphasis
upon the type of fan activity that they are most interested
in -- "geek culture", more interactive programming, etc. --
would lend support to the hypothesis that, should those

specific interests remain with this cohort, that those
interests will eventually find a place within the regional
fan-run conventions.

Fanzine Fans:

Those fannish fans who publish fanzines. It is still
too early to tell as to whether or not Fanblog (or
similar) fandom will fuse with fanzine fandom. I would
say that it is not going to happen really soon, though
I think it will occur -- except that the pace of
technological change may produce something that
supersedes both.

Traditional Fans:

AKA Old Fandom, Trufen, dinosaur fandom, etc. Are
fannish, most pub or have pubbed fanzines, and
they hold true to the norms and values that were
normative of SF fandom in the mid-1970s and
earlier. While it is possible that new blood will
enter into this subset of fandom, it is highly
unlikely given traditional fandom's attitudes and
less than inclusive nature. With hope, this small
subset of fandom will continue to survive in some
form; after all, it was the original form of SF
fandom.

And there we are. To cycle back to Issue #9; are the four male
leads in the US sitcom The Big Bang Theory genre consumers or
fans? I would say that they probably are, just barely (even
Sheldon), but that they would not be viewed as being fannish fans
within any present definition or worldview of what a fannish fan
is -- that is, within any **present day** definition.

So those are the working categories or ideal types for my
research.

Thrashing Trufen: "traditional 'fannish' fandom"

James William Neilson

The Canadian SF Fanzine Archive (mentioned last issue) has the stated goal of "celebrating traditional Canadian science fiction 'fannish' fandom". I promised last time to examine this statement, so here we go.

In the editorial of this issue I restate my categories. Using this as a guide, let me deconstruct traditional fannish fandom. A traditional fan is by default a fannish fan, all traditional fans are fannish. They tend to be engaged in fanzines, if not pubbing, in writing, or LoCing, or they have done so extensively in the past. They tend to be consumers of primarily literary SF over media SF -- they prefer written SF to SF films, television, etc. They maintain any local traditional fan community that may exist. They continue to participate in the old-style exchange culture of traditional fans. And some, very few, still reside in "slan shacks" -- shared accommodation arrangements with other traditional fans. However, this is certainly a greying group within fandom, the young whipper-snappers being about age 65 to 70 -- dependent upon geographical location. I say dependent upon location as there would seem to be differing degrees of inclusiveness from this fan category dependent upon region; the more exclusive traditional fans are in their locale, the less probable it is that there are any traditional fans within that local community who are under the age of fifty. Traditional fandom does not appear to be bringing in any new blood; however, I would be happy to be corrected on this (and to know what regions in the world this is happening in) as it would be shame for this category of fandom to die out completely. It would also be a subcultural loss if this category of fandom were to be redefined by the majority outside of it.

While all traditional fans are fannish fans, most fannish fans are not traditional fans. In addition, traditional fans may deem

fannish fans as being unfannish according to their criteria.
Bottom line, like it or loathe it, is that majority does rule and
it is the majority that determines definitional boundaries.
Thus, if a person is not a literary fan but they maintain a media
SF website/blog/etc. and they participate in volunteering and/or
organising local fan-run conventions; they are fannish (no matter
what the traditional fans may say). They engage in fan activity,
just not the entire set of fan activity that defines a
traditional fan. Just what constitutes fan activity is
determined by the majority of fans within a given region, who are
also engaged in fan activity, and that definition of fan activity
and fannishness will be mutable over time, usually becoming more
inclusive approaching the present. As stated in the editorial,
what is unfannish now, may be fannish in the future (certainly
the mediafan described above -- changing the website to a fanzine
-- would not have been defined as being fannish 30 years ago in
Toronto). That is the thing about fannishness, it is provisional
and rooted in the context of a particular geographical area and
place within time.

Thus, the danger of re-definition of traditional fandom by the
majority. It is very probable that in twenty years time that
that future majority may define traditional fandom as being those
people (in their late sixties and up) who still cling to the
traits common within fandom during the 1980s and 1990s -- i.e.
those people who came of age in fandom before the rise of social
media. You know, those old-timers who used to be on SF fan BBSs
and who posted on UseNet forums had their own websites and
archaic stuff like that...

And fanzine fans... Well, almost all traditional fans are also
fanzine fans, and the exceptions are few. But not all fanzine
fans are traditional fans, though all fanzine fans are fannish
fans. And it is uncertain that fanzines will continue to
survive. Again, they may as a small niche, amidst whatever is
the dominant form of communication down the road. They will be
electronic, like most are at present, and will probably be
available in whatever the dominant ereader format is (probably
something that is open standard and that you can read on any
portable device.

However, the trend is that what is now a traditional fan will be redefined and today's fannish fans will be redefined as tomorrows traditional fans and that literary fandom will be a niche within a greater fandom that is more inclusive. The greying of fandom has been the subject of much discussion since the recent Worldcon and not just the greying has been commented on, but also the fact that fandom is still predominantly male and European-descent. I.e. old and not diverse, see Lester's column. Fannish fandom, which this applies to, needs to get over itself and adapt to the new situation, which is; you are no longer the majority.

Literary SF is no longer the dominant variety of SF. Fannish fandom is no longer the dominant form of fandom. Thirty years ago, the more inclusive literary fans were making some niche programming available at conventions for media fans. Providing a place for them within literary fan conventions. Conventions like Ad Astra today are doing the same, while still a literary convention (based on GoHs), the line has been severely blurred, from a 1983 worldview, which is why I see this as a literary/media fan-run convention that is making the attempt to include to make a place for the interests of the under 30s (or is it now the under 40s). But, this will not work in the long run as the "youngsters" have numbers on their side, so making a place for them will not satisfy. That is why they are creating their own conventions (just as the mediafen did thirty years ago) and why these conventions are getting larger numbers of attendees.

A convention like Ad Astra will go one of two ways; it will have to become a smaller convention as its fannish fan audience dwindles or the executive will bring in new blood (most likely after the convention really looses money in a big way), young blood, who will completely transform the convention. It will still be fan-run but will only have niche programming for those who are defined as fannish fandom today and only niche programming for literary fandom.

A convention such as SFContario is a literary fan convention that doesn't aspire to be a big regional con and still attracts some traditional fans as well. I don't see this convention disappearing over the next decade, but I don't see it growing much bigger than it already is. Though it does have some

potential to attract some of the under 40s due to its size; a
small literary convention that offers the chance to actually meet
authors and talk to them as opposed to only queuing up to get
their autograph e.g. ComicCon or FanExpo. But it will never be a
big convention.

So, Graeme -- I have taken apart "traditional fannish fandom" and
concluded it is fading away. And thus, one of the major reasons
for the need of a Canadian SF Fanzine Archive and to celebrate
and commemorate what was fannish fandom as those of us middle
aged folk perceived it to be. Hence, my strong support for the
project. Though, I speculate that fannishness will continue in
the future, it just won't be fannishness the way it is currently
defined.

Pissing on a Pile of Old Amazings

...a modest column by Lester Rainsford

Lester recently read, in the introduction ~~of~~ to a (newly-published) cyberpunk anthology, some quotes of what Bruce Sterling wrote. Bruce wrote these incisive observations in his own fanzine back in the 80s. The observations are still as cutting today. Well, Lester hereby commits to <u>not doing any such thing</u>.Modern life is perplexing enough without some wiseacre columnist saying the things which you, by goolly, wish you had thought of first.

Speaking of modern life, or maybe perplexing, Lester and **The Swill** had a confrence, let's call it the Long Branch conference due to the ~~propiquinity~~ proximity of the TTC loop and GO station of the same name. Lester was Churchill and **The Swill** was Stalin, or was that vice-versa? No one ~~on~~ wants to be Roosevelt: dead too soon. Which reminds Lester that another ~~diatribe~~ exposition on TTC routes and Long Branch loop is well overdue, given that major changes resulted in through Queen car service back in 1993 or so. Alas, this column probably does not have space for such an important topic; another time maybe.

Back in issue 17, Graeme comments on a past "Pissing", that one should "never assume a reader is au courant in SF lit". Hence Lester's warning that one should carefully avoid virtual reality stories, which are an au courant trop in SF today. Well, fair enough, Graeme can now doubly avoid VR and save himself some valuable reading time to read something more valuable. However, it is a bit worrisome that old ~~type~~ time fans might be cheerfully ignorant of ~~th~~ what is being written today.

Look, Lester stopped by the skiffy section in Lillain Smith library (also home of the Merrill collection). The skiffy section is a big one, certainly biggest in Toronto, which means biggest in the known universe, what with Toronto being the centre of the universe etc etc. Uncer "Z", there were considerably more books by Sara Zeittel than there were by Roger Zelazny, and the Zeittel were mostly nice new hardcovers, while many of the Zelaznys were

battered old paperbacks. The lesson here is clear: the newere
stuff is what newer fancs are reading, possibly by preference,
but almost certainly by availability. For old time fins to be not
even trying, a wee bit, to be au courant just means that old time
fans are talking about stuff that's just not relevant to younger
fans. Whether that's old fandom feuds or authors you need to hunt
ip in musty second-hand stores. So at least a token effort to
keep up with that is au courant might go a long way to being able
to talk in new fan's language.

That being said, Lester firmly believes that new fancs, at least
of the literary side, read "The Science Fiction Hall of Fame"
because there are a lot of imaginative stories there. Stories
that are not quite conceivable today, kind of like the edicarian
life found in the Burgess shales is not quite concivable today
either.

There's nothing wrong with being a 20th century fan, nor to be an
observer rather than a participant (probably a theme with Swill,
eh wot?). After an admission like that, though, there's no place
for "why do the young fans not follow tradition" kind of
questions. (Which, to be fair, Lester does not fully detect in
Gareme.)

Finally, since this has already run overtime, Lester has
something to comment on from Immortal ConFusion. There was a
panel with a name somethink like "Diversity in SF", and was in
one of the BIG rooms and was pretty fully. So the whole thing
started, and after a minimum of introduction, a womoan on the
panel said "SF is totally diverse and welcoming". To the assorted
gasps from the audience, wshe said, "You become an sf fan by
working at conds, and if you come and volunteer for a con, you
will be accepted. Cons will accepty anyone as a volunteer."

Lester may be paraphrasing a bit freely, but that was the gist. A
riot then broke out....well no, unfortunately. The woman, who was
obviously a senior fan, and quite white, pretty munch maintained
here "you becomd a fan by working for a con, and anyone can
volunteer to work for a con, therefore SF is totally open and
welcoming" line.

Thing is, even if Lester agreed with her chain of logic (he does not, as a matter of fact), a quick head swivel in the panel's audience showed a very large number of white poeple, plus a couple of what Lester guesses are called "African Americans" in the states, as well as an oriental (author?). The fact is that congoers con-goers are not a particularly diverse crows, even in a suborb of Detroit which is famous for arab and Iraqi populations (Lester drove down to Warren for falafel type meals). Lester assumes that con-goers are a more diverse crowd than con organizers, although that is an assumption. SF is a pretty white sort of thing, and at least in the panels and events that Lester attends, is a white an aging sort of thing. Lots of white and grey hair, and entirely too many beards.

Lester would guess that genre consumers are a bit more diverse than "active fans", but even there, it's probably pretty white. There are all sorts of people on the streetcar (which runs to Long Branch, of course), and some of them are reading SF, but most of them are....white. Although young. (Lester does not necessarily approve of their reading. Lots are reading Martin's big series, and most of those are reading one of the first books. They should excape while they can!) (Lester geve up partway through the second book, aand has no regrets.)

Since we are taling about old time fandom, Lester was the death of Frederik Pohl is a sad event. Lester recently read "The Way The Future Was", and went to Fred's blog. There's the RIP note. Fred died September 2nd. Not only was he as old-time a fan as there was, he was blogging up until the day before his death. That's probably the baest way for a fan to go, with boots on....and apparently having pretty much finished a seuel to The way The Future Was. Lester looks forward to reading it. RIP Fred.

Flogging a Dead Trekkie: Violating the ~~Taboos~~ Norms of Science Fiction

Part 3 of 8 – Introspective Tales

James William Neilson

Malzberg's Taboos of Science Fiction or in my terminology, Norm Violations. These are story concepts and/or plots that if written -- if the norms are violated -- are unpublishable; no professional editor in the genre will touch these stories with a three-metre pole, and certainly would never, ever publish them.

NORM VIOLATION TWO: Introspective Tales

"Material which is highly internalized. That is, science fiction written from the point of view of a meditative and introspective central character whose perceptions are the central facet of the work, whose reactions to the events of the story are more important than the story itself."

Okay, I like this kind of stuff. I really don't see why this is hated so much other than it is hard to write an introspective tale that is also an action piece. If all you want is a pure action-adventure space opera, or a Campbellesque problem-solving story, then an introspective protagonist is really going to turn you off. As I said, I enjoy this type of story. I think that this type of story has strong value. I think that it is this type of story that raises the genre to high art. And it is also the type of story, like anything else, that you don't want a steady diet of -- everything in moderation and all that...

Norm Violation Two is also very similar to that of Norm Violation Four -- there is some cross-over here. And the usual response is

-- where's the story? Because, in the classical sense, there isn't one, or there isn't much of one. The science fiction approaches realistic mimetic fiction (aka mainstream) but it ceases to have plot as its prime driver. It may also ask or demand more from the reader, which is not a horrible thing at all. However, if the intention of the reader is to chill out after a long day of mental exercise at work; this type of story may be an unwelcome surprise and could end up posioning the well for any future stories of this type or from this particular author. Especially if it has been hyped in the back cover blurb to seem like it has a classical plot -- false advertising really ticks people off. Therefore, for short fiction, especially within the magazines, editors will tend to not opt for this kind of story as it can produce negative subscriber reaction. Anthologies can be kinder, dependant upon theme...

So, what about my story? Well there are two stories, maybe three, that would fit under this violation -- though one violates both Norm Two and Norm Four, so we'll save that one for later. The one that best fits Norm Violation Two is doubly evil it; it contains two different introspective tales that are only the most tenously linked to one another. The story also has mild undertones of Norm Violation One and a slight pinch of Clarke's History Lesson (just a miligram at the most). As far as the webstats go, not a lot of people read SWILL, so I am probably not damaging the experiment by providing the story title, which is Making Stones.

Making Stones has already been rejected by Market #1 and Market #2 an currently resides in a slushpile with Market #3.

The Title of my Norm Violation One story is Taking Care of Business which is currently out at Market #2 having been rapidly rejected at Market #1 -- they did not like it at all. More progress on the experiment next time...This story is currently out for consideration at Market #1 and I will report on its progress next time.

Scribbling on the Bog Wall:
Letters of Comment

James William Neilson

As I write this, there are one and one half LoCs this time
around. My comments are, of course, in glorious pudmonkey.

1706-24 Eva Rd.
Etobicoke, ON
M9C 2B2

August 28, 2013

Dear Neil/Jim:

Many thanks for Swill 18...it's taken a while to get to it, given I
am still frantically job hunting. Something has to give soon, and
I hope it's not me. Anyway, a few comments to try to fill a page.

In this province, my main documents like my SIN card, my birth
certificate card and health card do not expire, but the plastic
eventually rots. I could use replacement cards for each of these,
but it's a giant cash grab for the province, and the health card
will need to be renewed periodically, as opposed to the red and
white one I've had forever. There's also a non-driver's licence
ID card I'd like to get, but that's a cost as well.

Well my new Quebec birth certificate has arrived -- it is a piece of paper,
unplasticiesd, that I am NOT to plasticise or laminate and that should I
do so, this action would void and invalidate the document. Oh, and on
top of that, the birth certificate makes absolutely no attempt to make it
difficult to forge and thus, would be easier to forge than my old expired
birth certificate. SHRUG

The City of Toronto was also forcibly amalgamated some time ago,
with the idea that taking apart a level of government would save
a lot of money. It didn't happen, because that one level of

government was replaced with regional councils. I live just down
the street from the old Etobicoke City Hall, now the Etobicoke
Civic Centre, where the council meets. This costs even more now,
and there was never any savings to begin with.

Same thing here in Hamilton, except the old City of Hamilton, was
strongly in favour of amalgamation and was glad that the province
rammed this through. SIGH... We will see what happens with the
campaign, but the province will not budge on this issue and only an
NDP government might, possibly but not probably, be open to
discussion.

That's one thing I noticed...I started my fannish/SF reader career
with hope and aspirations for the future, and at some point, or a
particular age, the hope and aspirations went away, the future
looked more dystopian than utopian, and we started being more
reminiscent of the past, the good old days. More than just SF
fans go through this; I am sure we all do. Reality reared its
ugly head, to be sure, but I wonder if there is a particular
point when that happens, and what the circumstances are to cause
it. Very true, government is less for the public and more for the
corporations, as if we were fountains of unending amounts of
money.

It looks dark right now and who knows, we could still end up with a
Gibsonian cyberpunkesque dystopian corporate society sliding down the
tubes to total environmental collapse; we may also turn the whole thing
around and create a completely new global society that is more utopian
(by our standards). Nothing is determined yet. I am a cautious optimist
-- though the current trends do indeed point to dystopia...

I still read SF, though, but I have a pile of unread books on the
shelf, and I am more willing to ditch a book that just isn't
entertaining me than I used to be. Even legendary names in the
genre get back on the shelf when they are dull. Perhaps I need a
new genre when reality gets really ugly, and I need to forget
about it for a while, and take a mental vacation.

Personally, I am all over the map. In my fiction reading: right now I am reading A Turn of Light by Julie Czerneda and also Heinlein's The Moon is a Harsh Mistress (I didn't start with the juveniles so I didn't read much of Heinlein and someone told me the whole plot of this novel before I got around to reading it when I was younger; anyway, I am reading it now). And I have some British SF to catch up on as well...

My loc...I must have been pretty pissed off by some of the things I read online that day. I still want to see your results and reasons. I have heard of a new literary SF convention in Montreal coming up next year, and I hope I can be there for it.

Your tour dates...we weren't at Fan eXpo, but we will be at SFContario 4 (we have a vendor's table) and Ad Astra. We hope to be at the London Worldcon...the Texas Worldcon starts tomorrow as I type. And, I think Reversed Polarity is a one-shot convention celebrating the 50th anniversary of Doctor Who, so I don't think there will be a second one.

Yeah, I didn't think it would take too long for Montreal to form a new literary con. I won't be attending Reversed Polarity -- is this the last gasp of TCON? I will be attending the London Worldcon (don't know if for two or three days) as our trip to the UK is to see friends who live in the north of England.

Made the page, so I am done. See you with the next issue, and I hope this makes it in time.

Yours, Lloyd Penney

Okay Lloyd, will see you at SFContario -- the next ish will be out in time for that con. Plus, on Friday night there will be a SWILL party...

In the section eFanzines received, Felicity reviews Swill @ 30 #11 where she says,"...it sounds like there was some bullying in the original Swill, which still seems like a bad thing to me. For fairness, I read Swill #2 to see for myself, and it makes much more sense if you take it as good-natured punk sadomasochism than if you take it at face value. I guess it depends on whether you feel included or excluded by the zine's attitude."

Bullying, I remember that. So much fun... The joy of been beaten up every day at school in grade six. Why; because I was a "traitor" and a "frog" who had committed the heinous crime of being born in Quebec, that the core French that I learned in Montreal was light parsecs ahead of what was being taught in Ontario, that curriculum in the Quebec school system back then was about one year ahead of the curriculum in Ontario, that I was a Catholic attending regular public school (due to the timing of the move, my parents couldn't get us into the local Catholic school for that year). And to top it all off, this behaviour was supported by the school principal whom I recall my father referring to as a "fanatical Orangeman". Yeah, I know bullying; only they had a different term for it back then, patriotism. I really don't think that SWILL was bullying. Though, in the worldview of 2013, it probably would be to some people -- to which I say; whatever.

Just for the record, the people involved in the original SWILL (and the two of us still involved in the current SWILL) were not the "in-crowd" or anywhere near the centres of fannish power, back in 1981. We did attack the elitism of the self appointed trufen as well as any attributes that we associated with them (e.g. The Average SF Fan article) and we used an 90cm brush to spread our tar with -- collateral damage occurred and innocents/semi-innocents may have been harmed in the process. While this was an unfortunate occurrence, in the spirit of SWILL (then and now), our official response is: "Grow a backbone and get off my lawn!"

Just one small point, this review is appearing in the September 2013 issue of BCSFAzine for an issue of SWILL that came out in January of 2012. You do realise that 7 issues of SWILL have come out since issue #11 (issue #19 will be out in a few days time with this review as a LoC in it)?

Anyway, hope all is well out in BCSFA-land, and from the Lord of SWILL a big hello to all I once knew out there (Surrey Contingent Rules Okay)...hoping to snag another precious Elron again this year.

Endnote: Demographic Snapshot

James William Neilson

So, just some general notes on the first survey as well as from coded participant observation fieldnotes. The majority of survey respondents were people who attended SFContario and Ad Astra with a very small amount of Polaris attendees and still none from Fan Expo. Therefore, the current data is skewwed toward Fannish Fans with virtually no data yet collected from Fans.

The results mirror Lester's column this ish.

The average SF fan today is a European-descent, 42 year-old, male, married, without kids, with a post-secondary degree or diploma, who earns an average of $63,000 per year, who is an early adopter of new technology, and tends to read science fiction and fantasy just slightly more than they watch it, who reads over 20 books per year and watches at least 4 hours of programming per week within the genre, whose primary fan activity is to attend conventions and they attend at least 2 per year, they have never been a member of a SF fan club or organisation, just barely (50.6%) view fandom as a way of life, they have never published a fanzine, and they have been involved in SF fandom for at least 20 years.

So, thus far, I am only capturing the responses of those who have been long-time fans, most of whom -- like myself -- are greying. I am not getting data from the younger crowd, period. I think that I shall get one of my comsci students to design a survey app for release -- it seems that even an online survey is not catching the under 30s...

Okay, that's it until next time...

(Backcover, Portrait of the Anthropologist as a Young Droog #2)

SWILL

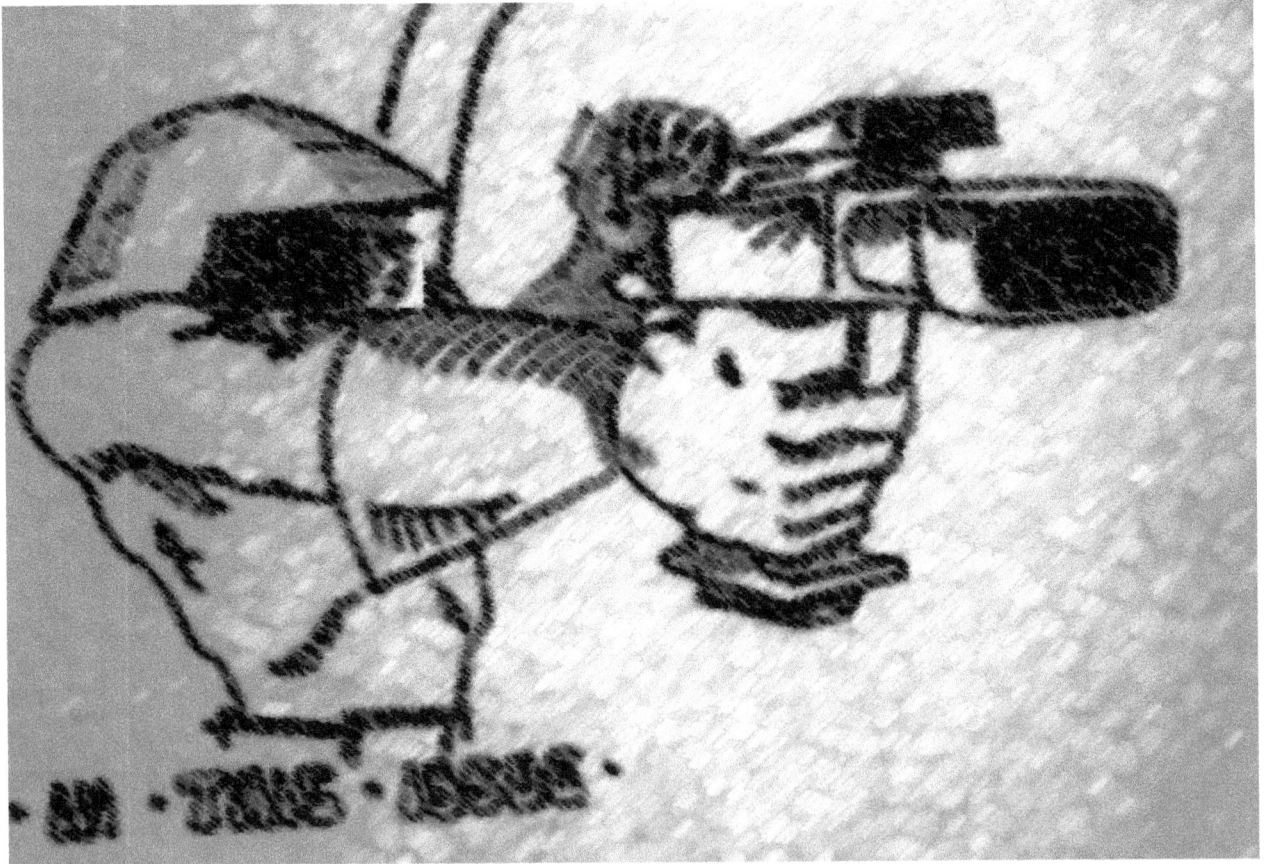

· IN · THE · ISSUE ·

#20   Autumn — 2013

Table of Contents

Front cover art by Rob Murray and Barb Winkler 1975 for Sirius #1; modified by the editor. Back cover photo taken in 1979/1980 by unknown and originally published in Miriad 2; modified by the editor.

SWILL is published quarterly (Spring, Summer, Autumn, and Winter) along with an annual every February - in other words, five times per year.

SWILL

Issue #20 Autumn 2013

Copyright © 1981 - 2013 VileFen Press

a division of Klatha Entertainment an Uldune Media company

swill.uldunemedia.ca

Editorial Of Fanzines, Archives, and Other Things...

James William Neilson

I had planned a rather brief editorial this time around, as the Special Feature in this issue is rather lengthy, centred around this being the twentieth issue of SWILL, and stuff like that. But then, Issue #40 of Fanstuff came out and I decided to devote this editorial to the issues raised in the first half of Fanstuff #40.

First of all I want to thank Arnie for his definition of SF fandom that appears on page 2. This is a brilliant lexiconic model that I really like; it has been created by a well respected member of Traditional fandom and it is non-judgemental. Here it is verbatum...

There's More Than One Kind of Fan

"Fan" is the most treacherous word in Trufandom's dictionary. Its multiple meanings, depending on the context, makes it a guaranteed fire-starter.

Even in our own subculture, relatively few fans puzzle over definitions. Non-fanzine fans are even less likely to have any interest.

The pertinent definitions:

• Definition 1: An enthusiast. Science Fiction and Fantasy are now part of mainstream popular culture. Just about everyone likes it in some form and approximately 80 million Americans identify themselves as "fans."

- Definition 2: A participant in Fandom. There are roughly 250,000 people who engage in some form of activity within the context of Fandom.

- Definition 3: A member of the subculture that is a direct, lineal descendant of the Fandom pioneered by such as Ackerman, Tucker and Speer. Robert Lichtman, the Sage of Fandom, calls this definition "us." Much briefer, true, but liable to more confusion.

They're all "fans," allowing for the context, but they aren't the same. Even if lexiconography is not your favorite pastime, the definitions should prove useful when reading the rest of this stuff.

Definition 3 fans are also known as Traditional fans, Trufans, etc. The majority of people involved in publishing fanzines are Definition 3 fans, though there are Definition 2 fans who are also involved in fanzine publishing, and I would speculate that there are also a scant few Definition 1 fans who may publish fanzines -- though, this activity would tend, if they persist in fanzine publishing, to transform them into either Definition 2 or Definition 3 fandom. There is also a cline or continuum of diversity within the Definitions; high levels of diversity within Definition 1 and Definition 2 and lower levels of diversity within Definition 3. That is expected as Definition 3 defines the sub-subculture of fandom that shares a traditional set of cultural norms and values, with some regional differences.

As for myself, I would place myself as being for the most part a Definition 2 fandom (Graeme would agree with this, though Taral and Lichtman would not), who has also spent about half of my fannish life as a Definition 1 fan. When I am active as a Definition 2 fan, I usually exhibit moderate to high fanac -- during my highest level of activity out in Vancouver, I pubbed fanzines, edited a clubzine, was a member of a sf fan club, did con organising work, panels, and was involved in the Ether Patrol -- (at present I would say low to medium-low fanac), and when I tire of that, I GAFIAte and become a Definition 1 fan. As I have stated previously, I am more a FIJAGDH-guy than a FIAWOL-guy. Perhaps, if my spouse was a Definition 2 fan, that might be different, but she is most certainly a Definition 1 fan. However, I have never been a Definition 3 fan; nor, do I think that I ever will be...

My fanzines are not and never shall be Definite 3 fan fanzines. Within the context of Definition 3 fandom, I am not, nor have I been in the past, fannish enough and I have never demonstrated the traits of a faan. Bottom-line, as stated previously as well, as a fan, my focus has always been upon the genre, and the ideas an concepts raised by the genre. I have never, as a fan, had a primary emphasis upon fandom itself. For example, as a fan, I always viewed faan fiction as boring and a waste of time. I don't read it, ever, as entertainment -- I only read it at present, wearing my academic hat, as part of my research (Sorry folks, it is still not my cup of tea). All of that said, there is nothing wrong (in my opinion) with Definition 2 fan fanzines -- though, I am certain that a zine like SWILL does not warm any hearts within Definition 3 fandom.

Onward...

I had some private email conversations with Graeme after he sent out his Open Letter. In short, I thought it was a great idea and made available what little I still possessed to contribute to the archive. The Open Letter raises many issues, but I would never say that "they've broken" Graeme. I would say that Graeme wrote the letter to vent and to promote the archive. He is not broken, after all, he is now a fandom columnist for Amazing Stories (a far more prestigious gig than being a columnist for SWILL; I really do understand Graeme and support your decision).

Graeme is frustrated in his, and others, lack of success in promoting fanzines to Definition 2 fans. I was on a panel last year with Christopher J. Garcia and Taral about fanzines at SFContario (a literary fan convention) and there was only an audience of maybe eighteen people (not counting Lester Rainsford). If that is a the draw at a con that still attracts some Definition 3 fans, then I am not surprised that the panel outnumbered the audience at a convention like V-Con. So, how do you promote fanzines? My thoughts are that you don't promote them as being one-and-the-same as Definition 3 fandom (face it, pubbing zines is such cultural meme to Definition 3 fandom, that once someone becomes a member of Definition 3 they will pub or contribute to fanzines). You promote fanzines by placing emphasis on it being unique, time-bound (issues as opposed to continuous), flexible (due to being time-bound you can have one theme this issue and a different, or no theme the next), and fun. A fanzine doesn't have to be a Definition 3 fan activity and it doesn't have to be fannish, but you do have to enjoy publishing your own zine.

Fanzine publishing is less immediate than a blog or a tweet, even for online zines (like this one). The younger the fan the more they are used to immediate responses to their activities -- minutes to hours. They find an interaction rate of days way too slow and would balk at an interaction rate measured in weeks or months. The majority of those under 30 are going to opt for social media oriented modes of interaction for their fanac (unless they are Definition 3 fans, but even here, they would maintain the traditional ways and also engage in the modern ways as well). Both Graeme and Arnie place emphasis on show-not-tell, but with different solutions.

Arnie suggests a hands-on approach that involves participation. In other words, a group activity at a club meeting/party to produce a one-shot, or perhaps a workshop at a 3-day convention that produces an apa-like one-shot. This is a good strategy for "(t)here's nothing like seeing Your Words in Print to spark up interest." I would also recommend using current technology in these activities. While a mimeograph and electric typewriter could attract interest, most of that interest will be for the archaic technology, not for fan publishing. Anyway, however you do it, hands-on participation is a way to attract interest.

Graeme has suggested an expanded fanzine archive that is online. This rather makes sense as a Graeme suggestion, he is one of the premeninent fan historians of Canadian fandom and the keeper of the archives of BC fandom. However, I disagree with Arnie; Graeme's suggestion does have merit. For me to visit any archive

in person, it would have to be a major collection, well
organised, and contain rare volumes that are only found in this
archive. As the goal is to attract fans and interest them in
fanzines, making the contents of the archive more accessable is a
way to spark interest. It is a more passive solution to the
hands-on approach, but it is a solution -- you at least now know
that fanzines exist and that they take many forms and styles.
Knowing something exists can be a spark to interest and
participation. Bill Burns' efanzines site does the same thing,
by making current fanzines more accessible and also providing an
archive/links to archives.

I also disagree with Arnie that "Graeme Went Wrong". The
Canadian Science Fiction Fanzine Archive is an ambitious project
that he describes in very excited tones in the Open Letter -- he
is in this document preaching to the converted and requesting
support and scanned content for the endeavour. Graeme and I have
not discussed this in any detail, so it is my opinion only, that
it is a passive form of promotion for fanzines. It isn't wrong,
it is a source of information, a source of information that may
attract some people to consider publishing a fanzine. However,
what it really needs is a how to page; show the uninitiated that
it is just as easy today to pub a fanzine as it is to pub a
fanblog (and far easier to maintain, SWILL had a blog for six
months, but it turned out to be too much effort -- pubbing the
zine only took up less time). Rather than right or wrong, both
approaches -- hands-on show-and-tell and archives of what's-been-
done and how-to-do-it-yourself -- are valid. I would also add
that Graeme's column on Amazing Stories may also serve to attract
increased interest in fanzines.

However, there will not be any renaissance in fanzines or a
return to the good old days of 1973 or earlier; fanzines are now
a niche within SF fandom rather than being central to it.

Another thing I want to discuss is the lament, mild but there,
that Graeme has focused on Canadian fanzine fandom and a Canadian
fanzine archive. While there are issues that cross the border
entirely or regionally, there are some differences too (and that
border is not as non-existent as many Americans claim it to be).
Graeme's goal is to create an online archive of Canadian fanzines

and Canadian fan history because, he is a Canadian. Anyway, if there is going to be an archive of Canadian fanzines, who better than a Canadian that is a historian of Canadian fandom. I wouldn't expect the Australians or the Austrians or the French or the Americans to create a definitive archive of Canadian fanzines and fan history. Obviously, it would be best if every national fandom created their own archives that were all linked via an international umbrella site, but you have to start somewhere and if there is going to be a Canadian fanzine archive, it should be compliled by Canadians.

And last, and in my mind, least... The issue of promoting or not promoting Definition 3 fandom, aka traditional fandom, aka Trufen. Obviously, as the editor of SWILL, I agree with Arnie that Definition 3 fandom should not be promoted -- though my reasons for this are, also obviously, different than his. Now, I am just going by my region (southern Ontario) here in Canada -- though I frequently tar and feather all Definition 3 fen everywhere with the same brush (this is SWILL after all) -- but based on what I have experienced over the years in my region of Canada, Definition 3 fandom perhaps deserves to die out and join the choir invisible. Definition 3 fandom cannot grow, because it is exclusive, judgemental, etcetera -- it was that way in the mid-1970s when I was in my teens and it appears to still be the same today. They definitely need to dump the old "fakefan" shit if they want to have any hope of attracting new blood and from what I've seen, they aren't all too interested in bringing in new members. Definition 3 fandom, in my region, is its own worst enemy and a potential albatross for attracting interest in fanzines.

Graeme, discusses (thoroughly and deservedly tolchocks in a SWILL-like fashion) the shortcomings of Definition 3 -- traditional fandom (self-appointed trufandom) -- in Space Cadet #23. He says:

> Trufandom has long been described as "the least welcoming fandom."

In all my years of promoting trufandom and seeking
converts I have been repeatedly rebuffed by SF fen who
adamantly refuse to listen to my pitch; some because
their previous experience and contact with trufen have
soured them on traditional fandom forever, but in most
cases because the one thing they know about us is our
reputation, and that alone condemns us.

Collectively we have the reputation of being the
biggest assholes on the planet...

Here's why:

All too often our message comes across as:

"Hi there! I see you are into costuming / gaming /
comics / filking / model making / convention running
/ SF movies / SF TV shows / SF novels / SF art / SF
whatever… What a dumb piece of shit you are. So
passive. So shallow. So stupid. So mundane masquerading
as a fan. Why don't you stop being a shithead and
become a REAL fan? We're the ONLY fans in the Solar
System. THE ONLY LEGITIMATE FANS. Join us. Or be
condemned to Hell forever."

And he does go on beautifully thereafter. Graeme and I are
largely in strong agreement on these issues. Our only point of
difference is that I think that the traditional fen of Toronto
have taken exclusivity and assholery to the level of a high art
form. Though, that could just be because they are Torontonians,
who view Toronto as the centre of the universe (which is
incorrect, that point is located on the site of the Albion Hotel
in Guelph, Ontario) and the rest of us Canadians are mere
peasants from the provinces (isn't that correct, Lester?).
Graeme tends to see this as a near universal trait in amongst
traditional fen with no major regional differences.

While Arnie may consider me to be a Definition 2 fan (and Taral
and Lichtman would classify me as a Definition 1 fan -- at best)
Graeme may consider me to be a Definition 3 fan (in some small
degree).

And thus, it is revealed at last and the mystery solved... I am
a Definition 3 fan, therefore I am a trufan, and thus a supreme
asshole and a fuckhead; hence, the publication of SWILL.[1]

---

[1] This would also mean that I must suffer from self-loathing of my wretched
trufan fuckheadedness...

Special Feature: The (Nearly) Definitive History of SWILL

James William Neilson

The History

The origins of SWILL lie in a surreal, last minute, idle prank.
It was October of 1980 and I was attending York University in
Toronto. My old high school friend, Lester Rainsford, was also
at York. Another friend of ours from secondary school, Andrew
Hoyt, was studying at the University of Ottawa. So, since I had
been to Maplecon in Ottawa the year before -- some other friends
and I had entered the masquerade as droogs from A Clockwork
Orange and won best group costume -- and had a good time; I
thought that Lester and Andrew might enjoy attending the
convention. Both were science fiction readers, but had never
attended a convention nor had shown any interest in fandom.

When Lester found out that this was going to be a science fiction
and comic book convention, he initially had cold feet about
attending. He said that we should do something about the comic
book fans. We bounced around some ideas, but none of them stuck.
Then, I showed Lester a "Boycott Chicago in '82" flyer, and he
said that we should distribute a boycott flyer at Maplecon III.
I told him that that would be pointless, since anybody who would
read the flyer would already be attending the convention. His
reply was, "Exactly." And thus, days before the convention,
Lester and I bashed out the boycott flyer on my aging manual
typewriter. The flyer was offensive, outrageously politically
incorrect by present standards, with intentional poor grammar,
typos, misspellings, and strikeouts. We printed 500 copies and
headed off to Ottawa.

At the convention, Andrew and Lester quickly became bored. They
found the panels to be dull or stupid, the dealers' room to be
overpriced and a waste of time, and the art show to be laughable.

By Saturday morning they were pretending to be sociology graduate
students from the University of Toronto gathering initial
research on deviant subcultures -- comic book fandom being highly
deviant and science fiction fandom simply deviant. Then Andrew
noticed that the boycott flyer was creating a stir.

Initially, we were putting out the flyers in piles of twenty.
These disappeared quickly, so we started putting them out in
piles of ten. These vanished even faster. Andrew and Lester
noticed that every time some of the boycott flyers were set out,
someone wearing a special coloured badge -- I forget the colour,
but it was the colour that indicated that the person was part of
the convention committee -- would spirit away the entire pile.
And so began a game of cat and mouse.

We started putting out flyers in piles of five, then one. The
convention committee eventually stationed somebody to watch the
table. Tape was borrowed from the front desk and the flyers were
put up in several places on the convention floor and in some of
the panel rooms. Now there was some poor sod patrolling the
entire convention floor searching for our boycott flyers. We
split the remaining flyers and distributed them in various
places; underneath other flyers, on the hotel literature and
tourist info table, in two locations within the hotel bar, and at
various room parties.

When Lester and I got back to Toronto, we discussed putting
together a one-shot fanzine for the Worldcon next year in Denver
that would be a whole zine of material like the Maplecon
Slandersheet. This one-shot was given the provisional title of
Up Fandom. November and December came and went as did the
semester. Up Fandom sat on the back burner as September 1981 was
still far far away. I toyed with the idea of putting out a
perzine and Lester perfected his score on Missile Command. After
Christmas, we both returned to uni and I attended the monthly
Toronto fan gathering/party in January.

It was at this event that I learned that the local powers that be
-- the Big Name Fans of Toronto -- were looking for who was
responsible for the boycott flyer. It appeared that the Ottawa
fan organisation that hosted Maplecon was very upset about the

flyer and that they held OSFiC responsible (well, we did sign the
flyer as "The Ontario Science Fiction Club, the motherfuckers").
The Ottawa Science Fiction Society was up in arms, they had
threatened (or so it had been rumoured) to sue OSFiC for damages,
and other crazy stuff. The Toronto BNFs who hosted this monthly
gathering took all of this very seriously. At the January
gathering the BNFs were interrogating anyone who had attended
Maplecon III in an attempt to find out who did this. Of course,
I claimed that I saw nothing, knew nothing, etc. and my old
droogs -- who attended the con as Nostromo crew (I think) -- who
knew that I was responsible, said nothing.

The next day when I reported this to Lester; who found it to be
hilarious. It was insane that OSFS could actually believe that
OSFiC actually wrote the Maplecon Slandersheet and even more
ridiculous that, even if OSFiC did write it, that OSFS would
believe that OSFiC would be stupid enough to sign their name to
the flyer. And so, the germ of SWILL was born.

Our first thought was to ramp up the timeframe for Up Fandom so
that an ish would be ready in time for the February gathering.
But then, I decided that this was just going to be a one-shot to
out ourselves for the Maplecon Slandersheet and to give a big
one-finger salute to the Toronto BNFs; why waste the zine name Up
Fandom?[2] And so, we named it SWILL.   It was eight pages in
length (okay, six pages if you don't include the front and back
covers) and we printed off maybe 20 copies of the zine (the first
print run was on photocopier which was a tad expensive) and 30
copies of the slandersheet, which I brought to the February fan
gathering.

Where, the shit hit the fan, so to speak. All the BNFs were
very, very angry with me. But they didn't actually say anything
to me -- that was how they displayed their displeasure, by no
longer speaking to me. Whatever I heard was second or third hand
at best. In part, the BNFs of Toronto were relieved to some
extent. I wasn't not in the centre of the Toronto fan community
and certainly not a traditional fan -- the only fanzines I had
pubbed contained mostly original amateur fiction (and one even

_____

[2] As it would turn out, there never was an Up Fandom zine.

contained some Trek fan fiction) -- and I also associated with
known reprobates (such as the droogs) who were card-carrying
mediafen (my droogs did actually also read SF literature, but
were very interested in media SF - two of them did end up working
in the industry). Nevertheless, the faanish members of the
Toronto community now declared me an "evil one" -- they were
angry, they disapproved, they would no longer talk to me, but
they didn't ban me from attending future monthly gatherings.

So, I enlisted the facilities of a friend in Guelph who had an
electrostenciler and a mimeograph to print a second run of issue
#1 and the remaining Ontario issues of SWILL; mimeograph was
cheaper and gave SWILL that grunge look that so befitted it.
And, based upon the BNF reaction, we decided to do a second issue
of SWILL.

Issues #1 through #4 were printed in Ontario and came out
regularly one a month for February through May. Then two things
happened: I moved to Vancouver and there was a Canada Post
strike. I moved to Vancouver in late May, arriving there just in
time for V-Con with a bundle of SWILLs. By the time I had fully
settled in and sent out the call, by mail, to get Lester and
Andrew to write some material for the next issue, there was only
one or two weeks left before Canada Post went on strike on June
30th. The strike lasted until August 10th and so, there was no
SWILL published.

Before moving to Vancouver, the plan was that there would be a
SWILL East and a SWILL West; Lester (as Arne Hannover) would edit
SWILL East and I would edit SWILL West. Both SWILLs would share
some content -- my editorials would be reprinted as a column in
SWILL East and Lester's column in SWILL West would be the
editorial in SWILL East. Looking back, this was a rather French
organisational design that probably would have failed in
execution. And then, there was the postal strike and BeSwill.

Steve Vano (Stephano) had already begun publication of his own
version of SWILL, BeSwill in April and by the time I left the
province there was a new issue every week. BeSwill really had a
very different tone to SWILL. Yes, it was obnoxious; yes, it was
crude; however, it really was not a SF fanzine in any way shape

or form. That is because, at the time, Steve really wasn't much
of a science fiction genre consumer; he was more of a gamer. So
in reading BeSwill one notices this, that there is a distinct
lack of knowledge of the genre that the zine is supposedly
critical of and even less knowledge regarding fandom. BeSwill
continued during the summer of 1981 and disappeared in the autumn
of that year.

In late August, I published a Worldcon Special Edition of SWILL
(which it would appear that I designated as whole number 5) that
we will now refer to as SWILL #4.5 and was a very short issue;
just a front cover, a back cover, an editorial, and a reprint of
The American Weigh. I don't know how many copies I printed, but
I probably made at least 100 that I brought to Denver along with
copies of SWILL #1 through #4. I do recall that people were
uncertain as to what to make of this fanzine in the Fanzine room
at the Worldcon. With hope, someone out there still has a copy
of the Wordcon Special Edition -- and if they do, would you
please scan me a pdf...

In late September I published SWILL #5 and in late November
(maybe early December) I published SWILL #6. Both Lester and
Andrew were getting too busy to supply me with regular material.
The major reason for SWILL -- ticking off the Toronto BNFs -- had
faded as I no longer lived in Toronto. There were actually
people who liked SWILL in Vancouver and I was getting more and
more involved in the anti-arms race peace movement and the
anarchist community to spend time on SWILL. The drive and the
desire had faded. As of February 1982, SWILL was no more.

In 1984 I published three issues of a fanzine called Daughter of
Swill, Mother of Scum. This magazine had some of the same spirit
that was in Swill, but it was also quite different. Each issue
was an essay on a single topic; one on fandom and fascism, one on
the science fiction of winnable nuclear war, and one on the lack
of alien aliens in science fiction. These were distributed to a
select group of friends. Of these three issues, the one on
science fiction aliens was the best. Again, no known copies of
this zine -- however, it you are reading this and do own a copy,
please scan it and send me the pdf.

In 1991, I wrote the fanzine Scum. It had a series of essays in
it on various topics about the genre and one on fandom. Some
reprints of old SWILL columns, such as Lester Rainsford's rant
against Libertarian Party science fiction, The Average SF Fan
article, and others... Also, there was some material that had
been written for SWILL by Hoyt and Rainsford, but never
published. I wrote Scum, but I never printed it off and sent it
out. It and all the SWILL related things went into a box in the
basement, where it would languish until a persistent, but
undetected, basement leak in that area reduced the SWILL box and
some of my wife's boxes of collected cooking magazines into a
mass of black mould that had to be properly disposed of.

In 2001, Swill Online was published as a website (still there at
http://members.tripod.com/swill_2001/). I had hoped that Lester
and Hoyt would write something for the website, but they didn't.
Swill Online has been designated as SWILL #7. Swill Online made
the first use of the pudmonkey font as the official SWILL font
(no longer supported on the original tripod site). About 20
copies of SWILL #7 were printed and set out on the fan table at
Ad Astra 2001. These print copies also contained a back cover
that was a boycott Ad Astra 2001 flyer. Unfortunately, a copy of
that flyer is no longer in my possession, but it had a similar
tone to the Maplecon Slandersheet.

In 2011, I revived SWILL as a fanzine. This is our thirteenth
issue since the revival began. SWILL won the 2011 Elron Award
for Worst Fanzine and it won the 2011 Faned Award for Best
Fanzine. SWILL continues to be published...

SWILL Contributors

Neil Jamieson-Williams (Neil Williams)
    James William Neilson
    Neil Williams
    Vladimir Schnerd
    unsigned

Lester Rainsford
    Illy Litrate
    P. I. Leninski
    V. I. Lenininsky
    Alicia Longspear
    Scrotum the Unbathed
    Arne Hannover

Andrew Hoyt
    Tim Parker
    Count Eric von Schicklegruber III
    David White
    Reginold Planetage

Steve Vano
    Stephano
    J.R.
    Ruby Beroach

Pete Roberts
    A Science Fiction fan
    G. O. Dowright
    Private Parts

J. S. Goobly
    Neil Williams & Lester Rainsford

Reverand B. Jeramiha Jones
    Neil Williams & Lester Rainsford

Scrotum the Unwashed
    a York University English Literature Professor

Rainbow and Kurt Kohl
    themselves

SWILL Issues

February 1981   SWILL #1

Cover Art: Neil Jamieson-Williams this was a badly drawn self
caricature of Neil holding a bottle of beer in his left hand and
a cigarette, while giving "the finger" with his right (the

"stubby" beer bottle is not well drawn and the perspective is off so it actually looks like a pill bottle).   Neil is wearing a T-shirt that says, UP FANDOM - the originally planned zine title for this intended one-shot.   Title composed of punk-style newspaper headline cut-out letters.   Editorial by Neil; article by Neil called MediaFen Suck; Pissing on a Pile of Old Amazings by Lester Rainsford; Fun and Games (Thrash the Trekkie) written by Scrotum the Unbathed and reviewed by Neil and Steve Vano; a reprint of the Maplecon Slandersheet; some fake LoCs; and the back cover - same as the front cover.

March 1981 SWILL #2

Cover Art: Neil Jamieson-Williams and Lester Rainsford - depicts three piles of shit, the one in the foreground labelled "Fandom" with lots of flies circling around it (preferred by more flies than other forms of shit).   Editorial by Reverand B. Jeramiha Jones on smut in SF and SF fandom; an article by Jamieson-Williams on Fen Art; Pissing on a Pile of Old Amazings attacks cigarette smoking and the discipline of Chemistry; article by J. S. Goobly titled The Average SF Fan (the infamous fat fan article); article by Jamieson-Williams titled They Space Tribbles, Don't They advocating the death of OSFiC; the very first Stephano My Fame strip; P. I. Leninski The American Weigh: Or, A Gram of Brains is Worth a Pound of Shit which attacks Libertarian Party SF, Libertarian Party SF Fandom, and some of the determinist claims made by the political philosophy of the Libertarian Party; actual real LoCs - only one is semi-fake which is a SWILL writer to writer response; back cover that proclaims that Physics Rules OK.

April 1981 SWILL #3

Cover Art: Kevin Davies - depicts Darth Vader in the Death Star trash compactor reading SWILL #2.   Title is also by Davies and would become the standard SWILL masthead.   Editorial by Jamieson-Williams on Del Rey Books advocating a boycott for the following reasons: classic reprints are overpriced, new authors are insipid, but most of all for the "self-destruct book" - Del Rey (at the time and least for the books shipped to Canada) was using a substandard adhesive for binding its paperbacks so that

the pages would fall out as you read the book. Pissing on a Pile
of Old Amazings (Rainsford) discusses the lack of original ideas
in science fiction. Articles by Alicia Longspear, G. O.
Dowright, Count Eric von Schicklegruber III, and Illy Litrate.
Endnote editorial about the purpose of Swill - Jamieson-Williams
denies that the purpose is to be nasty and obnoxious for the sake
of being nasty and obnoxious - is to offer critique to both
science fiction & science fiction fandom, albeit in a manner that
is often nasty and obnoxious but not without humour. Back cover
by Rainsford that is part of a SWILL contest.

May 1981 SWILL #4

Cover Art: Jamieson-Williams - "No Name" cover based upon Loblaws
No Name house brand of the time: 1 SWILL 12 GRAMS NEW. Editorial
by Jamieson-Williams on the disconnect between the future
imagined by SF fans of the 1930s and 1940s and the world of 1981
(no World Union, no abolition of war, no fair redistribution of
resources, no real conquest of space). Pissing on a Pile of Old
Amazings (Rainsford) discussed the TTC and cycling in the Caledon
Hills. Hoyt as himself bemoans the fact that the science fiction
section is filled with Star Trek and Star Wars and other
television and movie tie-ins but little real SF. Science or
Fiction by Steve Vano. Twinkle Twinkle Little Laser by Count
Eric von Schicklegruber III defends the discipline of chemistry
as being as important as and more relevant to the average person
than physics. Review articles by Stephano and Illy Litrate,
Marginal Phun by J.R., LoCs, and an Endnote by Jamieson-Williams.
In the Endnote there is the announcement that there would be a
Swill East and Swill West - Jamieson-Williams was moving to
Vancouver. Arne Hanover (Rainsford) was to head up Swill East
while Jamieson-Williams would edit Swill. Back cover by
Jamieson-Williams

August 1981 SWILL #4.5 WORLDCON SPECIAL EDITION

Cover Art: unknown (would have used the Davies masthead and may
have been a reprint of the issue #3 cover art). Editorial by
Jamieson-Williams that argued that the Worldcon should be called
the Americancon - the convention had a mostly US focus with few
international fans attending. Furthermore, at the time, only a

single Worldcon had taken place in a non-English speaking country. I also viciously trashed the Baltimore in '83 bid as I was a supporter of the Australian bid. Reprint of The American Weigh: A Gram of Brains is Worth a Pound of Shit. Most of this print run was distributed at the 1981 Worldcon in Denver and the remainder in Vancouver. Again, I have no copy of this issue and I am going entirely on collective recall.

September 1981 SWILL #5

Cover Art: Vaughan Fraser - shows an alien sitting on a toilet, every sheet of toilet tissue is labelled Swill. Editorial by Jamieson-Williams Viva, Maplecon that illuminates the relationship between Maplecon and SWILL -- Maplecon III being the catalyst for SWILL - and some of the early history of SWILL (this editorial was a primary source for the early history discussed in this article). Jamieson-Williams also does extend an olive branch of sorts to Maplecon 4 as they are no longer also a comic con and have returned to being a SF fan convention. There is a column by White thrashing tween and teen fans (most of whom are mediafen), a column by Hoyt on Star Wars, a book review column by Reginold Planetage about a fictitious book. Some LoCs from Ruby Beroach, a new cartoon by Jamieson-Williams (Star Captain Bruce), an endnote (sort of) titled After the "Worldcon" that takes back the nasty things said about the Baltimore bid (which actually won) and restates that the rest of his argument remains sound and stands. The back cover is a reprint of Maplecon Slandersheet.

November 1981 SWILL #6

Cover Art: Unknown. No copies of this issue remain, so this is all recall - as good as that is. I know that I brought some home with me for Christmas and gave a copy of this issue to Kevin Davies at a party and I remember that he wanted me to stop using the SWILL "masthead" that he created for the SWILL #3 cover and to stop crediting him in the zine (Kevin was starting to get some decent contract work as a SF & F artist and no longer wanted any association with a zine such as SWILL). Kevin also criticised my own strips - Star Captain Bruce - as being shit. I know that the issue he was talking about wasn't issue #5 as there were at least two Star Captain Bruce strips in the issue. As for what the rest of the content was in this issue; I have no recall. This was the final issue of the original SWILL.

February 2001 SWILL #7 Swill Online

For the twentieth anniversary of SWILL I created a website called Swill Online. Cover Art: by Jamieson-Williams (a cut and paste photoshopped image of a voodoo doll wearing a propeller beanie with R.I.P. written on it and a knife through the heart labelled "Fandom"). An editorial by Jamieson-Williams on why create Swill Online - to tease fandom. The State of the Genre states that it is very healthy thank you very much so stop whining and complaining. Is There Anything Unique About Fandom argues that there isn't. A Brief History of Swill is a partially correct and partially erroneous as it was written entirely on recall sans any primary source documents. In the Endnote Jamieson-Williams states that the site would be updated irregularly over the year and hoped that some of the old SWILL columnists and contributors would send in some material. They didn't and thus the site was never updated.

SWILL @ 30 SWILL #8 through #12 2011/2012

When I revived SWILL as an online fanzine, my original plan was that it would be a continuous issue, and that new content would just be added to the zine in almost a blog-like fashion. But after the launch of the fanzine and February I started to receive some LoCs and thus the only update to the very original issue #8 was a new column Flogging a Dead Trekkie where I ditched the original concept and went back to the traditional fanzine format of individual issues. Cover Art: A man in a chemical suit wearing a bowler hat sitting on the steps leading into some sort of containment area, with an umbrella tucked under his left arm and an open 650 ml bottle of beer in his hand. I used tweaked the original picture to make the man look more droog-like and make the umbrella sort-of look like a willy wacker and performed further modification on the photo. This cover art was then colourised for each season. Lester Rainsford rejoined SWILL for issue #11.

SWILL #13 through #17 2012/2013

The SWILL @ 30 masthead is dropped and replaced with the original masthead from issue #1. Cover Art: Jamieson-Williams as Anti-fan (who oddly enough looks kind of like Guy Fawkes) holding a lit 19th Century spherical bomb. Again distorted for each issue to indicate the season.

SWILL #18 through #22 2013/2014

Original Issue #1 masthead remains. Cover Art: the original cover art of Sirius #1 with Jamieson-Williams face photoshopped in. Again, with modification representing each season. Back cover is a photo of Jamieson-Williams in 1980 giving his old pal Fritz a mild tolchock; with minor distortion effects for each issue.

And that, to date, is the (nearly) definitive history of SWILL.

Thrashing Trufen: Traditional Fan "Exchange Behaviour"

James William Neilson

Traditional fen when they gather, in small groups at literary SF cons, senior's centres, and long-term care facilities, wax near poetic about the "exchange culture" or the "exchange behaviour" of traditional fandom. Then, they either launch into nostalgia about the "good, old days" or into diatribe about how this subcultural trait is lost on the sloth-brained "fakefans" (everyone who is not them) of today. So what was this "exchange behavour" anyway?

Well, I cannot really speak of this from experience -- I'm too young; believe it or not. I do vaguely recall from my teens when I went down to Toronto to attend OSFiC meetings that it appeared to be something like this... A segment of the literary fan community, almost all, if not all, of the members being involved in fanzines, who formed a close-knit sub-community. Within that sub-community the members exchanged items of value or of fannish value; artwork created by members, writing created by members, books, labour, resources (mimeograph machines, stencils, etc.), expenses (collectively or co-operatively sharing the expenses of fanzine publishing, travel to and from conventions, crash space at conventions, etc.), and a system of general reciprocity (sharing costs of going out to dinner as a group, spotting members when they were short of funds, and other forms of trade and exchange). Kind of like a slan shack from the 1940s and 1950s without all the members living in the same place of residence. Within this sub-community, fans shared, traded, exchanged with little or no monetary transaction taking place.

This has, in the past (and maybe still today), resulted in traditional fans shitting on fans turned pro or semi-pro for now charging for their work that had once been freely exchanged. They would dis these people as being unfannish, say that they had never been true fans, just "fake fans" masquerading as fans, and so on. They would also engage in behaviour that could be classed as intellectual property theft (and was) that they would justify as being their fannish right as trufen to do. This activity didn't endear them to many writers and artists; Harlan Ellison has been very vocal about this over the decades (but then, what hasn't he been very vocal about...).

Anyway, this exchange behaviour was very closely tied to fanzine publishing, local clubs being the foci of fan activity, and so on. With the decline of fanzines being central to SF fandom, beginning in the late 1990s, this has resulted in a decline of exchange behaviour in fandom. It really is only practiced within fanzine fandom, and only within the traditional fandom segment (albeit a large one) of fanzine fandom. That's because, in the old days, it was relatively expensive to produce a fanzine. There was the cost of the paper, the mimeograph stencils, the ink, the postage -- it was a commitment to publish a fanzine. You were making a commitment to the SF fan subculture and paying for it out of pocket. It costs nothing (provided that you are doing so electronically) to publish a fanzine today, other than your time and labour. That old level of commitment is absent as is the need to share the burden of costs. And hardly anyone still published fanzines. The traditional fan exchange behaviour is slowly dwindling toward extinction.

However, I am uncertain as to whether or not I will mourn its loss. Just as I don't mourn the loss of rotary dial phones, black and white CRT television, and 8-track tape... It is something from another time and that time has passed.

Pissing on a Pile of Old Amazings

...a modest column by Lester Rainsford

Newsflash! This just in! Swill is a menace! Watch out for Swill!@ Swill will follow you home. Swill will disparage your cat, kick your ass, and drink your beer. Swill dispatches its myriad Pudmonkey minions to harass and appall peaceful happy zine publishers. Swill is a bully!!!

Well, no. Swill is a zine, not google, and even google can't do that. "Bully" is a popular term these days, and like many popular terms it's grossly misuesed.

Swill is a punk zine, okay? It's going to be obnozious and in your face and generally have an attitude. Lester thinks that Swill should be politically incorrect, only not in the way the Baen's Bar posters are politically incorrect. Swill is politically incorrect in the correct way! Ha, take that!

Truth to tell, Lester is a little relieved that readers found Swill obnoxious enough to mischaracterize it as a bully. Lester has a fear that Swill is not obnoxious enough. That it's really white middle-class pseudo-punk work. That a real punk would spit in the face of Swill, probably transmitting a number of interesting and undesireable diseases. So being called a "bully" is okay in Lester's books.

Now, come here, give Lester your lunch, and bend over for your daily bare knuckle scalp massakege massage, kid.

Elsewhere and a few issues ago, Lloyd P. opined that he preferred the hard galaxy-smashing stuff of the '60s and '70s, and found their that tech "harder" than today's nanotech etc. Sorry Lloyd, that's bunk.

Not that today's nanotech is particularly hard, but the galaxy smashing stuff in the '60s was abouty as hard as the latest Metrcedeys Lackey book, which is not hard at all. Lester has been increasingly pondering some of the hidden un-hardness of the tech from those days (and in today's SF too, of course). To do galaxy-

Osmashing (or spanning) you need starships with FTL drive. Well, hello not-hard handwavium! Ciao, bolonium!

Here are a couple of things that have Lester going "hmm".

1. Energy and fuel. Even assuming that a true FTL drive is possible, how can it take so little fuel that it seems no more onerous to power an FTL starchip than it is to drive your '67 Chev ~~Biscayne~~ Biscayne to the new plaza with the shiny K-Mart? The answer is, the fuel and energy needs are blithely ignored, in the interests of writing a story where shipping mangoes from Procyon to Betelgeuse makes some kind of economic sense.

Lester has a story idea here. Suppose FTL travel was feasible, actually possible, but as the ship went to FTL ~~tav~~ travel, the drive gave off enough hard radiation to sterilize the system it was leaving? Kind of a nice gamma-ray burst. Maybe this has been written as a story, in which case Lester would place it in the early 1970-s when all was gloom and we suck.

2. Ever wonder why the USS Enterprise pulls out of orbit before going to warp drive? Why the average SF starship needs to "get out of the gravity well" before going to hyperspace? Why not depart from low orbit, or in fact from the comfort of your living room?

Imagine a story written in ~~1995~~ 1885 about the exciting world of air travel in the future. To fly from Toronto to London (England), everyone boards the magnificent airplane, which is of course a flying boat, in Toronto harbour. The airplane motors down the length of Lake Ontario on its lake drive, and down the St. Lawrence to somewhere close to Newfoundland. Finally the magnificent air driver are turned on, and the flying boat launches into the air. For, of course, airplanes can only fly over the ocean.

See what's been done there? Instead of beinb packed on a small metal tube for a short period of time, staring at the dismally slow progress shown on the tiny screen in front of you, there's a chance for intrigue and character, what with the grizzled air captain, the sinister and scheming first mate, and the veteran air ~~flyer~~ hand with the parrot on her shoulder.

The whole "got to get away from planets for a distance" does the same thing for interstellar travel. It's all bolonium, but bolonium that's handy for the story. You can have your grizzled space captain with the tan from a thousand ~~south sea ports~~ suns, the sinister and scheming first mate, and the veteran space hand with the parrot on her shoulder. Arr, now we be talking good pulp ficition!

Lester has the theory that this model of interstellar travel really was the result of World War II. The US campaign through the South Pacific took a lot of SF writers on a trip to exotic hard-to-reach locations, but not impossible-to-reach locations. Sturgeon's "Killdozer" is based directly on his war experience, and James Schmitz was down there during the war too. Lester considers this to be adequate proof of his theory.

On Lester's to be re-read pile is The Last Heathen which describes a quest to ~~find~~ clarify some mysterious history from the 1800s in the South Pacific. While the writing isn't Vancean, the characters and backgrounds could be from a picaresque Vance novel. And Jack Vance was in the merchant mareine in World War II. ~~QWQ~~ED.

Hey, ~~punk~~ puke, where's the Oreo cookies in your lunch? Ya holding out on Lester? C'mere! Now!! Give 'em over and Lester will only beat you up a bit.

Flogging a Dead Trekkie:

Violating the ~~Taboos~~ Norms of Science Fiction

Part 4 of 8 – Unaccepted Mores

James William Neilson

Malzberg's Taboos of Science Fiction or in my terminology, Norm Violations. These are story concepts and/or plots that if written -- if the norms are violated -- are unpublishable; no professional editor in the genre will touch these stories with a three-metre pole, and certainly would never, ever publish them.

NORM VIOLATION THREE: Unaccepted Mores

"Science fiction which implies that contemporary accepted mores of sexuality, socioeconomics, or familial patterning might be corrupting, dangerous, or destructive."

In other words, science fiction that is critical of our present socio-cultural norms and values; even worse, those norms and values that we have attached a strong ethical and/or moral perception upon.[3] In other words, norm violations that actually may be societal taboos.

So what would be a violation of mores or taboos regarding sexuality in today's society? Depends on which society and what segment of that society. The old ones for our society, say back in 1980 when Malzberg wrote the 7 "taboos" of science fiction, would have been homosexuality, bisexuality, sadomasochism, bondage, and the like. These forms of sexual behaviour in

---

[3] That's what makes them mores as opposed to just norms and values, and a culture's most strongly held mores are also known as taboos.

contemporary Western society are either accepted (e.g. homosexuality and bisexuality) or tolerated to some degree provided that those involved are consenting adults. Violations in this regard are still viewed as taboos within certain segments of Western society, but these segments do not represent the majority any longer. Present taboos would when there is not consent or when the sexual behaviour involves adults and minors (in particular involving adults and minors in a relationship that is incest). That said, keep in mind that some of the minority segments within Western society that still consider homosexuality and bisexuality to be a taboo may not have a prohibition regarding adults and minors (including incest) - fundamentalist Mormons for example. Also, the definition of incest is also cultural; there are seven different systems of determining kinship that are practiced world-wide (each with differing determinates of what is incest and what is not). Marrying your Mother's Brother's Daughter is considered incest in our system, but would be the ideal marriage partner (i.e. allowed and encouraged) in another. Bottom line; what is a sexual taboo today and can we make sweeping generalisations for humankind as to what is and is not a sexual taboo. If it is not considered normative by the majority in Western society, it can still be viewed as at least a more violation should it appear in a story.

Question is; would this be sufficient to make the story unsalable? Maybe, or maybe not - it all depends on how strong the violation is and the tastes of the particular editor. I would hazard the speculation that if the story is well written, doesn't violate any of the other norms of science fiction, and provides a rationale as to why the fictitious society/alien species practices the particular violate of accepted mores, that the story would find a home somewhere in today's market.

Similar for familial patterns in a SF story. A lot has changed since 1980, same-sex marriage, single parenting, blended families, and so on. Living common-law was still not viewed as being normal in 1980, though it was, for most, not a violation of accepted mores; today, it is normative in our society. However, some things have not changed - few advocate crèche-rearing of children and those who advocate this are considered to be in violation of society's mires. Nevertheless, if you can write a great story and provide rationale as to why that society practices crèche-rearing of children, you can probably sell it.

One violation that has closed up from 1980 is violating socioeconomic mores; in particular any portrayal of a future society that is socialist or practices state socialism (e.g. the former Soviet Union). While the first two violations of accepted mores would have been a big problem in 1980, violating socioeconomic mores would have been an easier sell. After all, the alternative existed in the real world in the form of the Soviet Union and the Peoples' Republic of China. Writing stories where these forms of socioeconomics existed did not appear far-fetched or in violation (so long as the state socialists where the bad guys or if there was also societies that practiced capitalism). You would have been in violation of mores if you made the state socialists the good guys or if you used Marxist theory to demonstrate that the collapse of capitalism was inevitable. However, several US writers in the 1970s and up to the late 1980s were able to successfully violate this more in their fiction.

Since the Fall of the Soviet Union and the restructuring of China's economy to be mostly capitalist, any form of socialism is out in science fiction - in particular in the USA. The dominant view is that socialism, in any form, is a failed system that has been discredited and therefore has no place in any story set in the future; the use of socialism, especially state socialism, is viewed as a departure from realism and thus places the story on the borderland of fantasy, thus unsalable. This is different outside of the USA market to a greater or lesser degree. Essentially, the contemporary more is don't depict any type of socialist or anarchist society (unless it is an anarcho-capitalist society) if you want to sell your work in the American market.

However, you are permitted to write that secret societies, people operating in the black branches of government and/or industry, and so on are a menace or a threat in USA science fiction. Here, the good and wholesome free-enterprise capitalist system has been co-opted by a hidden elite and corrupted; so long as your hero(ine) intends to restore a nice, pure, democratic, free-enterprise capitalist system at the end of your tale. Then, you are good to go.

It is still heretical in the American SF market to claim that our current Western capitalist economic system - that claims that it is possible to have infinite growth within a closed and finite system and which depends on that growth to sustain itself - is unsustainable. Fact of the matter is, that without change and without "magic box" fully mature nanotechnology and/or bioengineering and/or AI arriving at the eleventh hour over the next 50 years, our current economic system will collapse. It is already under severe strain - the 2008 Financial Meltdown and Great Recession is still an ongoing "hot potato" bumping about in the pinball machine of the global economy; the root causes of the Meltdown were not resolved or fixed, they just put on a band-aide.

As for my story? Well actually one could say that Norm Violation One Story also violates Norm Three; Taking Care of Business is currently still out at Market #2. FYI, Making Stones is now at Market #4. My actual story that is the Norm Violation Three Story is a parallel universe tale that is in the slushpile of Market #1 and has the title Back in the USSR. Oh, by the way, When I say Story X is out at Market #1, I mean Market #1 for that particular story (Their Market #1 could easily be Market #6 for a different story).

Note to prospective editors: Not that I think any of you actually read SWILL, but who knows. I just want to state that, to the best of my abilities, these pieces of fiction are being written with serious intent - this is not a lark (otherwise, I would have ground out some shit and sent all seven out at once). Till next time…

Scribbling on the Bog Wall
Letters of Comment

James William Neilson

As I write this, there is only a single LoC this time around (yet again, from the usual suspect). My comments are, of course, in glorious pudmonkey.

1706-24 Eva Rd.
Etobicoke, ON
M9C 2B2

October 17, 2013

Dear Jim:

Thank you for Swill 19, and time to respond to it. I know these don't come out very often, but I am catching up with the zines I have, and might soon be totally caught up as long as I can write one a day.

We are all consumers to one degree or another, but more and more, I see people writing about the actors they met, the autographs they got, and not much more. We are being conditioned to become passive consumers rather than active creators. It will be interesting to see what happens to that current under-30 segment of fandom creating their own geek culture conventions as time goes on. They create their own version of fandom, just as we did.

Time will indeed tell. All that is certain is that the version of fandom that the under-30s will create will be nothing like old traditional fandom.

As for fanzine fandom, they still demand a certain level of trufannishness, one I am slowly but surely realizing as subjective and somewhat irrelevant. I have lost some face in their eyes as I look at other avenues of fandom, like steampunk, and even new fandoms, such as that being created around the popular Murdoch Mysteries show. (Already, MM fandom is starting to resemble the original Trek fandoms, as middle-aged fangirls squee over anything Yannick Bisson might say or do, and tell everyone what they'd like to physically do to him. Also, we have one member of this fandom who is making some of the cast and crew uncomfortable with he near-constant presence at shoots; we easily recognize her as the obsessed fan.)

The odd thing is that I really do believe that fanzines could have a larger niche within fandom; the biggest obstacle to fanzines is that most fans who aren't involved in fanzines viewed them (rightly or wrongly) as being one-and-the-same as being involved in traditional fandom. SWILL is not a traditional fandom sort of fanzine. And a fanzine doesn't have to be a traditional fandom sort of fanzine or buy into that sub-segment of the SF fan subculture. Now steampunk zines; I see that as a good fit to the sub-genre -- up to and including the printing of the zine on paper and mailing it out.

I never was a fanboy, and could never understand that behaviour that colours part of mediafandom. Then, as my wife (a stage actor) has noticed I don't usually remember the actors names in a film of television programme; just the character names, the plotline, arcs, and maybe the producers. I like media SF, but not to the point that I lift the actors, writers, etc to demi-god status.

I recognize myself in your description of the fannish fan, but as said above, I see it as increasingly irrelevant, especially as the seniors in this category reach their 70s and 80s. I hit a few BBSs in my time, and they were fun. Same with UseNet groups, and they have died out, I think. The same is happening with Yahoo! and Google Groups. I am looking a little further afield, and finding that there are a few steampunk zines, and I am trying my best to respond to those zines, usually produced by people who are further into this interest than I am. Literary and fanzine fandoms indeed need to get over themselves and say they are no longer in the minority. The results of this year's Hugo awards made that abundantly clear.

I think you actually mean no longer in the majority; and they are not. Yes; though I have changed the definition set once again. However, this time I am fully drawing upon that of native knowledge on the part of Arnie and Graeme. This is what I am going to remain with, except that I will keep the category of genre consumer (there are many people out there that consumer SF & F regularly but do not identify themselves as fans) while realising that the line between a Definition 1 fan and a genre consumer can be very blurred. Definition 3 fans -- traditional fans -- is a really a niche fandom, and a small one at that. All Definition 3 fans are fannish (many of them are faannish) and there are many segments within Definition 2 fandom who are fannish, but not in the manner accepted by Definition 3 fans. Bottom line is that fandom changes over time...

I don't think SFContario wants to be a big convention, but if it does want to expand a little, it will have to find a bigger hotel. Toronto has lots of big hotels and little hotels, but not much in between.

I agree. I like this con a lot for its size and scope and hope that it can remain close to what it currently is.

My loc…my job hunt continues yet. I know how difficult it is for anyone over 50 to get work, but I didn't know it was this bad. I found out the province has made getting their general ID card easier to get, but it is still $35, and must be renewed every five years.

Again, good luck in your quest...

I had thought that The Tcon Society would be staging Reversed
Polarity, and then going on to other projects, but it doesn't
look like it. Rumour has it it will simply shut down its
operations. I hope that's wrong, I think a smaller event could
work, and people are very much missing Polaris; there's a big gap
on the July calendar, and I am surprised no one's tried to fill
it yet.

I have heard the same rumour. I have taken TCON to task
(mildly – as, in a way, I don't really care) in my Endnote. Now
I realise that you do care, you two used to be involved in conrunning for this convention, correct? For me, the con is of
minor interest, as I am still a literary fan first and as said above,
I don't get into all that actor worship, etc.

Time to wrap, it's close to lunch. Take it easy, and see you at
SFContario 4. Thanks for the heads up at your party…

Yours, Lloyd Penney.

See you at SFContario :)

Endnote: Much Ado About Nothing TCON

James William Neilson

According to rumour, Reversed Polarity will be the last convention organised by the TCON Promotional Society. They are simply going to roll over and die in response to increased competition from Fan Expo and the fragmentation of fandom. This is, of course, their choice to make; I just don't think it is a good one.

Their reasons are:

- Increased competition from FanExpo events that can pull in bigger name stars that TCON can afford to do

- Increased difficulty in bringing in convention volunteers to assist in running the convention

- Increased competition from small fan-run conventions -- many of these aimed at the younger SF & F audience

- Shift in fan attitudes toward fan-run media conventions

These are all reasons to reconsider what you have been doing and make changes; they are not reasons for voluntary euthanasia.

In this time, when there is a major transition going on in fandom, one of the options is to put on a smaller convention (not an uber-relaxicon like Polar Chill). There is definitely a market in Toronto for a smaller fan-run media SF convention. It is time to re-think the convention, to reach out to those younger fans with programming and events that they are interested in, to change the way things have always been done. A convention model that worked well a decade or more ago will need to be adjusted for the present.

But, maybe the TCON executive IS making the right decision. Perhaps they are not equipped to transform the way they do

conventions. And if they are unable or incapable of change, then
now is indeed the time to call it a wrap and fade to black.

Pith Helmet and Propeller Beanie Tour

The face-to-face participant observation portion of the research
project is starting to wind down (PO will continue via the
internet, etc.). Here are the final tentative tour dates as they
currently stand...

November 2013 SFContario 4 -- Toronto

August 2014   Loncon 3 -- London, UK

November 2014 SFContario 5 -- Toronto

SWILL

· IN · THIS · ISSUE ·

#21   Winter — 2014

Table of Contents

Front cover art by Rob Murray and Barb Winkler 1975 for Sirius #1; modified by the editor. Back cover photo taken in 1979/1980 by unknown and originally published in Miriad 2; modified by the editor.

SWILL is published quarterly (Spring, Summer, Autumn, and Winter) along with an annual every February - in other words, five times per year.

SWILL

Issue #21 Winter 2014

Copyright © 1981 - 2014 VileFen Press

a division of Klatha Entertainment an Uldune Media company

swill.uldunemedia.ca

Editorial: Shit-Kicking Space Opera

James William Neilson

I love space opera -- it has always been one of my favourite
subgenres of SF. However, there have always been some very
crucial problems with space opera that never, ever, have gone
away; key assumptions that really, when you look at them closely,
make all space opera (even the not-so-new New Space Opera) rest
firmly within the realm of science fantasy.

First and foremost, realistically, space travel is going to be
difficult. Even interplanetary space travel will be hard. As
Douglas Adams stated so clearly and humorously decades ago; space
is really, really big... Even if we were to develop a spacedrive
that allows us to send out ships at a cruising velocity of .127
AU/day it will still take a fortnight to reach Mars at its
furthest distance from Earth (factoring in say 3 days to
accelerate and decelerate at both ends of the trip). Jupiter in
about two months (with longer periods of acceleration and
deceleration) and Neptune in about 8 and one half months, and the
Alpha Centauri system in about 6,000 years.

And this "realistic" spacedrive is still a lot of handwavium
bullshit -- I have just arbitrarily guesstimated how long the
ship is going to take to accelerate/decelerate and confess
without shame, that I couldn't calculate specific impulse, etc.
to save my life. And I haven't even discussed energy and fuel,
because in my head I have selected baloneium-based vacuum
energy/zero-point energy as the fuel source -- something you
don't have to haul along with you and I also haven't calculated
for ship mass empty or when fully loaded with passengers and
cargo. The sad fact is that interplanetary travel is not going
to be a piece of cake. Even if we go the route of aborted
Singularity magic box supertech brought to you by fully mature
nanotechnology and friends, it remains just a lot of more
"realistic"-sounding technobabble. In my teens, I used to feel
that Clarke was very pessimistic when he saw humanity still

poking about the solar system three to four centuries from now --
now I see this as very realistic.

So, even with my more "realistic" baloneium spacedrive, you're
not going to see any Solar Empire emerging even in our planetary
system; probably an Earth/Moon/Mars Empire and perhaps extending
out to Jupiter, but beyond; no. And even within a Jupiter and
inward Solar Empire, there will be areas that are hard to control
politically, like any asteroid settlements. But all that means
is how easy it will be to send out the Imperial Space Navy to
keep the colonials in line. We haven't even started to discuss
why there are colonists out there and what resources, etc, they
are providing that are dearly wanted back on Earth and all of
that...

And we are still just talking about our solar system. Any
possible interstellar empire is going to require FTL.

Lester had some comments about this last issue:

"Here are a couple of things that have Lester going "hmm".

1. Energy and fuel. Even assuming that a true FTL drive is

*possible, how can it take so little fuel that it seems no more
onerous to power an FTL starchip than it is to drive your '67
Chev Bicscayne Biscayne to the new plaza with the shiny K-Mart?
The answer is, the fuel and energy needs are blithely ignored, in
the interests of writing a story where shipping mangoes from
Procyon to Betelgeuse makes some kind of economic sense. Lester
has a story idea here. Suppose FTL travel was feasible, actually
possible, but as the ship went to FTL tav travel, the drive gave
off enough hard radiation to sterilize the system it was leaving?
Kind of a nice gamma-ray burst. Maybe this has been written as a
story, in which case Lester would place it in the early 1970-s
when all was gloom and we suck.*

*2. Ever wonder why the USS Enterprise pulls out of orbit before
going to warp drive? Why the average SF starship needs to "get
out of the gravity well" before going to hyperspace? Why not*

4

*depart from low orbit, or in fact from the comfort of your living
room?"*

Energy and fuel as Lester points out seem to be a non-issue with
FTL in space opera. But it should be a major issue as it is
going to take a substantial amount of some from of energy to
propel your protagonist's ship at superluminal velocities and
that energy is also going to have to come from somewhere. And
that whopping energy is potentially a hazard.

For example, we have currently developed an ultracapacitor for
use in an average sedan that would give 120 km/hr over a range of
350 - 400 km (and only takes about 10 minutes to go from zero to
full charge). Why is this vehicle not on the road? Because
people drive cars and people get in accidents when driving cars
and in an accident the ultracapicitor has a high probability of
discharging all of its stored energy at once. At full charge the
discharge would turn the vehicle into a fireball and make the
rear-ending a fully fuelled Ford Pinto seem like a minor safety
issue. Lester's musing about a massive gamma ray burst as your
ship enters FTL when leaving a system is exactly what is
theorised would happen when an Alcubierre drive ship drops out of
warp as it enters a system - not a very pleasant way to say
hello, but one certain to rid you of any difficulties with alien
lifeforms more complex than bacterium.

Now I know, and Lester knows, that his grumbling about having to
leave a gravity well to start up your FTL drive, is little more
than a plot device to place some sort of limitation on the FTL
drive or to give downtime for the main characters to interact
with one another before they jaunt off to the far stars.
Obviously for the later, there are different ways to accomplish
this without having several days/weeks journey before the FTL
drive can be turned on, and yes, this cliché does have its roots
in the experience of ocean travel of the middle decades of the
20th century - actually, many of the tropes in space opera
harkens back to the sea battles of the two 20th century World
Wars.

The former, is so that the evil alien hordes of Vlashirma Prime
have to drop out of hyperspace in the outer system and take a few
days/weeks to arrive in Earth orbit (giving the protagonist some
time to develop a plan). While I agree with Lester that the "no
gravity well" rule is arbitrary and can be demonstrated (as he
did aptly) to be nonsensical, I am in favour of placing limits on
FTL travel. Whether it is no gravity well, or must be close to a
gravity well, or that the ship must be travelling at a specific
velocity, or that there are specific points of entry, I am kind
of a supporter of this plot device, and I have used it myself. I
have come up with some unique variations over the years that I
haven't seen anywhere else...

The FTL drive has a 70 percent chance of vaporising the ship when
it re-enters normal space - which means it would not be used for
transporting passengers but insured cargo and the pilots would be
suicidal or deeply in debt or possibly both. Where ship's mass
is a limiting factor; a small 5 person crewed ship can travel at
twenty c but your humungous space dreadnaught can only trudge
along at maybe 1.1 times the speed of light. Or, my favourite,
the ship has no control once it enters hyperspace; it takes a lot
of energy to push the ship into the correct hyperspace current
where it drifts to the chosen destination and where the journey
for those aboard will take several weeks (zero time within normal
space). Again, these limitations are simply arbitrary and
reality may have already provided us with a limitation - FTL is
possible though you will sterilise your destination upon arrival.

The thing is about space opera - it is not hard science SF - very
little that is called hard science SF space opera actually really
does contain hard science. Oh it may have AIs, nanotechnology,
genetic augmentations, dyson shells/rings/swarms, and well
thought out FTL drives, etc. that sounds all technological and
scientific... But when you get right down to it, when you
examine it clinically, it just sounds that way; in reality it is
just technobabble for golems, magic, demigod powers, and magic
lands near and far that can be reached only by swift elvin ships.

Yet, in spite of these flaws, I do still love space opera.

Thrashing Trufen: Meeting the "Bad Boy" of First Fandom

James William Neilson

I in particular and SWILL in general, have been so-to-speak called up on the carpet, for being nasty and mean to traditional fandom in these pages; especially in regards to that sub-segment of traditional fandom who claim that they are the one true fandom. I don't know what benighted thoughts were going through the "minds" of those who envisioned that by attempting to scold me (as if I was a naughty child or subordinate) they would insure good behaviour in the future. Whatever they were thinking, they were wrong - 100% wrong. This is SWILL. You read SWILL the Riot Act and you will get a Molotov cocktail thrown your way. And neither I, nor SWILL the zine, is going to knuckle under to politically correct, social-worker platitudes to "play nice". Not only does SWILL have its own historic reputation to uphold; there is extra pressure to maintain our reputation now that we have met the "Bad Boy" of First Fandom and introduced him to SWILL.

Now the term "Bad Boy" depends upon whose side you are on from the early days of SF fandom. Regardless of side, though (and had I been alive back then and living in NYC, I would have been a Futurian rather than a New Fandomite), he has been a fannish figure who has disturbed the shit, on more than one occasion, and been a trouble-maker, at times, and been involved in fanzines, conrunning, etc. since well before either Lester or I had been born. At SFContario 4, Lester and I met the famous (or infamous) Dave Kyle - the creator of the 1939 "Yellow Pamphlet" that resulted in the "Great Exclusion" at the first Worldcon, Nycon I. We invited him to attend the SWILL party that was taking place that evening (Friday) and (echoing the events of 1939) pressed a copy of the SFContario 4 Boycott Flyer into his hands two hours before we began to distribute them at the con. Kyle (unlike what happened at Nycon I) kept the early release to himself and didn't immediately take it to the concom - not that it would be any secret as to who the culprits were as the flyer was written entirely in the pudmonkey font. Now, it is our understanding that some of the concom was pissed regarding the boycott flyer and the rest didn't care or found it fitting the fan GoH.

Anyway, it would seem that the fan GoH liked it, or at least the spirit of the flyer, as he said when he briefly popped into the SWILL party before he retired for the evening.

Lester and I made a point of attending his kaffeeklatch at 9:00 AM the next morning - both of us a little groggy as the SWILL party had been the last party standing Friday night/Saturday morning. It was at the kaffeeeklatch that Lester and I gave Dave Kyle SWILL 2011 and SWILL 2012 (the paperbound collections of all SWILL issues for those two years) and, of course, we signed the copies. I also talked to Kyle several times on Saturday and came to the following conclusions.

Here was a member of traditional fandom, a member of First Fandom, who while quick to launch into nostalgia and stories of the early days of SF fandom (that's why he was there as GoH) was not judgemental about my generation and those younger within fandom. Not at all -- any judgemental comments seemed to be directed at old adversaries (like Sam Moscowitz) but with humour and contextual explanation (for the actions of his adversaries) and without malice. And not a word about how those under 60 or those under 40 or those under 20 have "destroyed fandom". Now, he did use the term trufan when referring to traditional fandom a couple of times, but he was speaking in the context of the 1930s to the 1950s, with no subtext that this was when trufandom existed, never to come again. For all I know, he may have thought that and was too wise to actually say it; but I don't think so. Face it, Dave Kyle has had a long and full life; a life that has seen many changes in his soon to be 95 years. He has been a SF fan throughout his life and he wouldn't remain involved, even to his current minimal extent, if he wasn't able to adapt to the changes. I really do not think that he subscribes to the same worldview of the Toronto "Old Guard" of traditional fandom who view everyone under age fifty to be "fakefan" mundanes.

Oh, is he a fanzine fan -- damn right. There is no question about it. Is he interested in fan history, of course (he is walking and breathing fan history). Is he a social media, twitter-head, teen-love vampire fan? Well, I didn't ask that question, but would strongly speculate that the answer is a firm "No" -- though he has a Facebook page... Anyway, it was great to here him tell his version of fan history from the early decades, with a hint of mischief still in his eyes. I only wish he got the chance to finish telling the story (his version) of what happened when the Futarians found out he wrote the "Yellow

Pamphlet"... Nevertheless, both Lester and I received
reproductions of the original "Yellow Pamphlet" from Dave.

With hope, Dave will enjoy the SWILLs he received; and Dave, if
you're reading, you are always welcome to have your very own
column here at SWILL (No pressure, just if you feel up to it...).

Note: We apologise to BCSFAzine that the above column was not
befitting of SWILL's bully reputation. Don't worry, we'll give a
thorough thrashing to someone next issue.

Pissing on a Pile of Old Amazings

...a modest column by Lester Rainsford

In five years, science fiction will be obsolete.

Ha ha, Lester is just having a bit of fun. A whole pile of SF is <u>already</u> obsolete, and has ~~been~~ been for years. And a lot of what's left is irrelevant.

'Obsolete!' you cry, like somoene staring at a teletype that works no more. 'When? and how?' Well, space opera, and the whole general star-roving tales we're used to, became increasingly obsolete starting in the mid-2000s, and by 2010 you could put a fork in them. Yet the space opera part of SF keeps going on like a brontosaurus that's been attacked by a T Rex but not yet fallen over. The firs fangs went in prior to 2010, as discussed above, and by now T rex is feasting on the brontosaurus' liver. The brontosaurus meanwhile figures it's only chance is to ignore the T rex and hope the rest of the day gets a bit better.

A whole pile of space opera and star travel and the light of distant suns over a hardscrabble spaceport is based on two assumptions and a resulting question.

Assumption #1: there are a reasonable number of solar systems out there like our solar system, with some combination of earth, Mars, and mercury-sized planets closer to the star, and gas giants further out. Lester recalls reading simulations based on planetary formation models, and this is about what was found. In ~~as~~ addition many starts had low angular momentum, presumably gone into their surrounding planets.

Assumption #2: star travel is reasonably easy, or at least somewhat feasible, but not impossible. This is not scientifically valid, but let's go with it.

Resulting question: where are aliens? If there are lots of planetary systems, why ~~are~~ isn't there intelligent life on at least some of them? Combine with Assumption 2, and you have to wonder why the Groaci or the Posleen or the Regul havne't dropped by yet.

The question is actually Fermi's Paradox, and it's pretty old (and it's not exactly Asimov's Paradox, or Banks' Paradox). Fortunately it's an open-ended question, so there's lots of room to answer it however you want, and voila your plot is in motion.

Maybe there's something extra-unusual about our solar system and earth (like a very large moon), and therefore we are the only intelligent life. Well, the galaxy is mankind's! (Yes, it's a pretty Campbellian 'Man will inherit the universe' setting.)

Or, your story could be about first contact, which you do skillfully enough to palm the card that says 'but that should have happened back in the paleolithic' and, when no one is looking, throw it down the garbage disposal.

Or, maybe the aliens have been manipulating us all along. Lester can recall a few such stories, like some by Doc Smith, and maybe one or two by Philip Dick.

And then the astronomers had to come along and ruin it.

When the first few reports of extremely large planets in extremely close orbits came in, well it was pretty easy to dismiss that as "okay, we didn't expect that, but our detection abilites aren't very good. We have found a very wierd system, because that's the only kind of system we can find." The T rex was just a rustle in the bushes....

But as system after system was found, and basically none of them resembled anything we were familiar with, it became pretty clear that our models of planetary system formation were all wrong. Or maybe our models of how planetary systems work over time--there is evidence that those hot close super Jupiters and formed reasonably far out and then migrated inwards. Yes, Velikovsky was onto something! (Few astronomers will admit to this.) And the tRex was starting to dismantle the rib cage about then.

Don't even think about dark energy and dark matter.
Astronomers don't know what they really are, and the
implications are unknown (we're talking "unknown unknowns"
in Dick Cheneys' parlance).

If van Vogt was writing now instead of in the 1940s, you bet
he would come up wilth all sorts of wild stories where the
hero takes dark energy to twenty decimal places and becomes
superhuman with tendrils, or something. But today's SF
writers, a timorous and unimaginative lot, neither care to
cope with this, nor are able to cope. So the space opera
yard goods keep getting turned out, despite the fact that
the universe is not like that; even more, not only is it not
like that, it's stranger than anyone understands or imagines
at this moment in time.

A huge opportunity for creatinve and exciting stories. We
dont' have them. Lester, once again, suspects that the
series and yard-goods orientation of current SF is to blame.
If you don't really understand what's going on, you can play
with concepts in short storys and novelettes. However, if
you are turning out multi-book series, you stick with what
you know, and what you know is the two assumptions, and you
write. Like the brontosour, you hope that your day gets
better, and these pesky results will go away. In the
meantime, the T rex of reality burrows deeper into your
vitals. In five years, people will look back at current
space opera, and it will be totally obsolete, kind of like
stories that assume the Cold war with the Soviet Union is
still going on in 2113, or that there will be one very big
computer running on vacuum tubes controlling the world.

Well, Lester certainly hopes that this will be the case in
five years, but the momentum of ~~irrelevant~~ obsolesence is
very hard to stop. As Hari Seldon said (lester seems to
recall), when a brontosaur, or huge old tree, is very big,
it takes a long time to fall over. But when it does fall
over, boy does it make a mess. That's why Lester hopes that
it falls over sooner rather than later (pllus lester would
love to read some interesting new stuff in short-story
form). (Lester, too, choses to ignore invonvenient reality.)

The astute reader may have noted that, while some SF is
obsolete already, other SF is irrelevent. Lester will return
to that anon.

Flogging a Dead Trekkie:

Violating the ~~Taboos~~ Norms of Science Fiction

Part 5 of 8 – Mood Trumps Plot

James William Neilson

Malzberg's Taboos of Science Fiction or in my terminology, Norm Violations. These are story concepts and/or plots that if written -- if the norms are violated -- are unpublishable; no professional editor in the genre will touch these stories with a three-metre pole, and certainly would never, ever publish them.

NORM VIOLATION FOUR: Mood Trumps Plot

'Science fiction which owes less to classical, Aristotelian notions of "plot" - the logical, progressive ordering of events as a protagonist attempts to solve a serious and personally significant problem - than "mood".'

This is the type of story that leaves the traditional SF reader (and thus also the typical SF editor) complaining that there is no story. And they are correct, in a classical sense -- there is no central problem personal and/or otherwise for the protagonist to solve, i.e. no classical plot. The mood or atmosphere of the story overshadows the plot, and the plot tends toward the forms of stream of consciousness, a slice of life, and the vignette or vignettes. There is often no firm resolution at the end of the tale, or only a minor resolution. Instead, you get a portrait of the protagonist(s) and the world that they inhabit.

To which the average SF reader and editor are quick to say, "Fuck that literary fiction bullshit; give me some action, conflict, a climax, and some resolution, or else you can just piss off!"

Now, I do like stories where plot trumps mood, but I also like stories where mood trumps plot. I do not have any major preference overall, though stories where plot trumps do tend to be an easier read. However, what I really enjoy is in longer pieces (novellas and novels) when the author balances both, or at least alternates between the two poles. So, as a reader, I rather enjoy a good mood trumps story. I am not advocating a steady diet of this type of tale, only that I like it. And really, unless you are an action junkie, what really is wrong with the occasional mood piece?

As a writer, I am a frequent violator of this norm as well as norm violation two (introspective tales). I have also been guilty of these violations for many decades, even back in my radio days. The majority of my radio writing was 100% solid classical plot driven stuff, like the serials written within the subgenres of space opera (On The Rocks) and cyberpunk (Rhonda Riot and the Insurgents). But most of my miniseries (The Time Tracks Set) and single episode pieces (By the Shores of the Tranquil Sea) tend to have a greater emphasis upon mood. I am looking back to my time in radio, as evidence that it was not academe alone that influenced my constant violation of these norms; they were already present in my writing.

But, academics did push me further in that direction -- a good fieldnote excerpt within an ethnography should act as a portrait of the culture/subculture and/or the worldview of the people or a single person within that culture/subculture, their perceptions of, and reactions to, and the meanings that they attribute to the events that occur within the world that they inhabit. Thus, being a norm violator (in particular of number two and number four), although pre-existent, was encouraged and amplified in the course of my academic training. And this may be a stumbling block in my writing of short fiction (or at least a major detriment to selling that fiction) because I am a repeat offender.

Norm Violation One story, "Taking Care of Business", also violates Norm Two and may weakly violate Norm Four. Norm

Violation Two story, "Making Stones", also strongly violates Norm Four. Norm Violation Three story, "Back in the USSR" also violates Norm Two. Both of my Norm Violation Four stories engage in multiple norm violations; "Secondary Deposition of Cultural Remains" violates both Norm Two and Norm Four, while "The Last Children of Apollo" only additionally violates Norm Two.

So, there we are until next time. I will only report the progress of these stories should I happen to sell one of them (professionally).

Scribbling on the Bog Wall:
Letters of Comment

James William Neilson

As I write this, there is only a single proper LoC this time around (from, of course, Lloyd) and a couple of email LoCs (sort of) from Taral. My comments are, of course, in glorious pudmonkey.

1706-24 Eva Rd.
Etobicoke, ON
M9C 2B2

December 17, 2013

Dear James:

Thank you for the 20th Swill, and congratulations on getting the word out about Swill to the unwashed masses at SFContario 4. Great party, and greetings to Lester! Comments follow, and I hope they make sense.

Ah, but this is SWILL, Lloyd -- LoCs that are pure gibberish rants are always welcome (though it has been a long time since we received one of those) and "making sense" is never a requirement... But yes, the SWILL party was a success and there will be one next year at SFContario. I was toying with the idea of doing a SWILL party at Ad Astra, but couldn't get a room on the party floor (or in the Sheraton for that matter, I'll be slumming it at the Best Western).

There are fans of all stripes around, mostly because there are now so many different interests encompassed by the simple term

'fandom'. I think older fans remember a past time, and wonder
about all these new people with new interests, and aren't very
accepting. I may be guilty of this myself, but I do remember a
different time, and wish I could return to it. Traditional fans
seems to be a good term to use to describe that older crowd.

Okay, I am going to eat my previous words regarding myself. I
now do agree with Graeme, I am a traditional fan -- albeit an
iconoclastic and heretical traditional fan, but a tradfan
nevertheless. As I have mentioned before, my first involvement
in fandom was not with "real fandom" but with other science
fiction fans my own age in secondary school. When I
discovered "real fandom", the majority of the people involved
were tradfans and this really was the only fandom in the mid
1970s (other than Trek fandom). Even the non-Trek mediafen
of the late 1970s (and some of the Trek mediafen) had been
enculturated/socialised by tradfandom -- which definitely was
the dominant form of fandom -- into adopting many of the
norms and values of tradfans. Many, but not all.

I cannot recall that any of my fellow fans from that time period
had a burning desire to turn the clock back to the late 1950s and
live the fannish lifestyle of then. But we produced fanzines, we
ran/participated in the running of conventions, were members of
clubs/formed clubs, and participated in weekly/monthly fan
socials. That some of our fanac was deemed improper or not
"real fanac" by the uber-orthodox tradfans does not make that
fanac "unfannish" even in the temporal context of the late
1970s/early 1980s. And within today's context, it was
traditional fan activity.

As for the contemporary "young turks" of fandom and traditional fanac, more on that later...

I've tried to get friends interested in fanzines, but to no avail. They have their own interests, and I have mine. No renaissance for us, we are a niche interest, and that's the way it will stay, whether we like it or not.

I don't see any renaissance either. However, like Graeme, I see there being room for growth. Not big growth, just enough to sustain the niche. And that will require some tolerance on the part of the old guard. Any person under 30 who is drawn into fanzine fandom is entering in as a digital-native with full knowledge of all the internet and social media memes that they will probably attempt to port to the print medium in some form. They will experiment, etc. And that is to be expected. I experimented with audio fanzines in the late 1980s. When I first revived SWILL, I had an experimental model in mind that it would just be an evolving single issue that would grow in content as time went by -- kind of like a semi-static blog. That I changed my mind and switched to the traditional issue-by-issue fanzine format, says a lot about me actually being a tradfan. And where the Fanstuff set, and even Graeme, and I part ways is that I would view a multimedia fanzine that has a blog, podcasts, video content, and traditional print component as being a fanzine -- especially if it has separate issues.

Jump-cut to your next paragraph... Yes, I have seen a few of the steampunk zines and they are very good. I would not be surprised if some will actually be printed on paper (if I recall

19

correctly the old Dominion Dispatch first issue of each volume was only available in print) maybe even printed by mimeo.

Anyway, I have still not heard back from the programming gods of Ad Astra on doing a workshop on fanzines and an Ad Astra APA (digital, of course) at the con; but, there is nothing like hands on to generate interest.

My loc...I have expressed my opinions about fans being trained to be passive consumers, and lots of people have disagreed. They feel that there's plenty of people staging these new conventions, and creating podcasts and blogs. I have to agree with them, and see that they have their own activities. One old fannish phrase is The Happy Deadwood, those fans who did not participate in managing clubs or conventions or other fannish events, but who still put their money down to belong or attend or take part. Their cash is as important as any activity, for they help to make things happen, too. I am finding steampunk zines here and there...The Gatehouse Gazette, now ended, Steampunk Magazine, Exhibition Hall, Aether NZ, and recently, The Concordium. They are mostly if not all electronic zines, but the production values are just amazing.

Ah, I haven't done conrunning for a few decades, but I recall the term. Yes, the Happy Deadwood were your bread and butter as they would attend and spend money and their attendance was their fanac. The "young turks" are already holding their own conventions, etc. As an old fart, I can look back and say that this was very similar to the late 1970s and early 1980s when it was the fannish mediafen who were starting up the first fan-run media SF cons. The difference between then and now is that back then, this group was in the minority and today, they are a majority within fandom. Established fan-run SF cons need to tap into this group and their energy to revitalise their cons and bring in the younger crowd. That will mean some changes and the old guards running these cons will have to adapt. It also means that part of the nature of fan-run conventions will change dramatically. <SHRUG> Look, you either change so that new blood is attracted to attending your con or your con will eventually die (usually by the con going bankrupt) and the youngsters will create a new con to occupy the same niche in their own image. By bringing in the youth, you at least have some possibility of socialising them or having them gain an understanding of what older fans want to see in a convention -- it doesn't mean that they will listen or not go and re-invent the wheel, but there is a possibility. The fact that the "kids" are creating their own fan-run conventions is a good sign; it means that trade show cons like Fan Expo are not enough and that they do want the face-to-face social time that exists at a fan-run con. Current conrunners should be attempting to capitalise on this (says the anarch-syndicalist, fully aware of the irony)…

The job hunt…I did find work at an agency in Etobicoke, but the contract I signed will not be renewed in the new year thanks to a shortage of work, so I must look again. The TCon Society may be staging another Polar Chill with more programming in it. That's what the grapevine tells me right now. We were never formally connected with TCon, but Yvonne was the founder of Toronto Trek Celebration / Toronto Trek / Polaris. Her initial goal was to stage a Trek convention, but to bring in the script writers and book authors. Well, THAT didn't work… Many of the TCon people are right now quite tired. People come up to them with lots of ideas about what should be in the next convention, and from what I've seen online, they are quite tired, and would like to see someone else take over the reins, and run cons.

Good luck in the job hunt. Yeah, I did a few years of contract work. It sucked the big time with the constant insecurity, will the contract be renewed or not, etc. All I can say is keep at it, man...

Polar Chill with more programming may attract me to attend. I have little interest in attending a media SF relaxicon or actually any relaxicon these days.

If the TCon leaders are burnt out; see above. The con will change. It will tick off some of the older attendees, yes. But, if you want to sustain your con, you cannot only cater to an aging and thus, over time, dwindling population of attendees.

I'm trying to write as many of these letters as I can before the end of the year so I can get caught up on the pile of zines I have, either electronic or paper. Thank you for this one, and I hope you're working on the next one.

Best of Christmas and New Year to all.

Yours, Lloyd Penney.

Glad to hear from you, as always, Lloyd. I hope that you both had a wonderful holiday season and all the best for you both in 2014...

```
From:      Taral Wayne
Date:      Sun, December 1, 2013 5:08 pm
To:        swill@uldunemedia.ca
```

Graeme tells me he believes you intend to be humorous, but after
reading issue after issue on the same theme, I have come to doubt
it. So I have begun to lose my own sense of humour.

From: swill@uldunemedia.ca

Date: Sun, December 1, 2013 5:55 pm

To: Taral Wayne

I understand from Lloyd you have a missive for SWILL. Will
be happy to receive it regardless as to its humour.

As I said to Graeme; some of what we say is real and some of it
is humour. Bottom line is that I do not accept the notion that
only the "trufen" traditional fans are real fans and that all other
fans (the majority) are "fake fans". Didn't accept it 30 years ago
and I don't accept it now.

Neil


```
From:      Taral Wayne
Date:      Sun, December 1, 2013 7:04 pm
To:        swill@uldunemedia.ca
```

Yes, but nobody is saying that anymore. Oh, a few hold-outs like
Arnie, but no reasonable Old Schooler insists he's the only kind
of SF fan ... or gives a damn, really, what the hell fandom is or
isn't. Just because a person may be a Polish, left-handed or a
Democrat is no reason to regard them as your bosum buddy who you
welcome into your home. The collective identity is too large to
be meaningful on a personal scale. At the scale fandom has grown

to, it is impersonal ... and not worth investing a huge emotional
stake in.

So you are fighting against staw men, a battle far too easy to
win. It's over. Move on.

Well, I never received from Taral the missive Lloyd had
mentioned at SFContario 4. Anyway, here is my response to
Taral s second email.

Okay, now I do not know Arnie, but recently, it would appear
that he does now agree that fandom does include all fans, but his
preferred fandom is traditional fandom -- which he still insists
upon calling trufandom. My question is, have you also had a
recent sea-change in opinion on this subject. I do recall that
when we met at SFContario 2 and discussed the issue, that you
were of the opinion that only traditional fans were fans and that
SFContario was not really a traditional fan convention. Which I
disagreed with, as I saw the con and still see it as a small scale
primarily literary fan convention that definitely seemed to be
very tradfan from my perspective.

And I don t think that you agree with my definition (or
Graeme s) as to who is a traditional fan. I think that your
definition is more exclusive and linked to subcultural memes
that have largely disappeared. The whole concept of Fandom Is
A Way Of Life, that SF fandom is your primary social network,
that if someone says that they are a fan then that means that
they-share-common-norms-and-values-with-you is gone. It has

been gone for a long time, actually. If someone says to me that they are a fan, all it means to me is that we may actually enjoy the same genre in fictional entertainment (and even that could be wrong as they may actually be a fantasy or horror fan who doesn't like science fiction) and that is it. That doesn't mean that we will like the same type of SF or share an interest in the same SF subgeneres, or like the same films, or like the same television programmes, but we may be able to talk together about the genre.

Thing is, I am not looking for a new "bosom buddy… (to) welcome into (my) home." I don't see SF fandom as my primary social network, at all (even in secondary school when it was my primary network, it was that within the context of a particular secondary school and it was not my only social network, either). That said, most of my oldest friends are people that I met within the context of SF fandom.

From my perspective, upon which we do not now, nor have we ever in the past, agreed, you are an uber-orthodox or orthodox traditional fan. Your version of fandom has shrunk to a minority within traditional fandom and is but a miniscule niche group within all of fandom. And that shift from dominant majority to entering minority status began (in my opinion) circa 1970 with orthodox tradfandom becoming a minority between 1990 and 1995. It has never been my SF fandom and I have always been a FIJAGDH person, it is a part of SF fandom that will probably go extinct over the next twenty years or so (in the form that you like it to be).

And yes, you are correct; growth of the genre is what killed orthodox traditional fandom (as well as new technologies). The growth of the genre in the 1960s and the linkage to the sharp increase in fantasy (we're still talking about the literature, i.e. print) increased the number of fans. The penetration of the genre into other mediums further accelerated that increase as did the increased popularity of the genre(s). More readers, more viewers, etc. takes away the small village feel that your preferred type of fandom required; a type of fandom which can only be maintained within a self-imposed ghetto within the big multicultural city that is fandom.

Again, I don't mourn this change of fortune any more than I mourn the loss of rotary dial phones -- I don't have any emotional investment within this niche of fandom. However, I do not have any desire to lay waste to orthodox traditional fandom and smite it from the face of the universe. I will continue to poke it with a stick, especially when members continue to make claims that they are the one-true-fandom, for entertainment. You may not find being poked with a stick (especially when it is a pointy stick) all that entertaining (I understand that) but it is also a SWILL tradition, which means that I am going to continue to do it anyway.

Endnote: The SWILL Stance

James William Neilson

Notice to All Readers:

SWILL has been condemned for:

- being nasty and mean to traditional fandom (in particular those members of orthodox traditional fandom who continue to insist upon calling themselves "trufandom")

- being a bully to traditional fandom for over 30 years (we have also been mean and nasty and a bully to comic book fandom and media fandom in the past -- we remain, a partially, equal opportunity bully service)

- polluting the precious bodily fluids of fandom (we really don't want to know more about this nor do we desire clarification...)

- associating with "known reprobates" (and we will continue to do so)

- and probably some other offenses/fannish crimes...

The official SWILL stance to these accusations is as follows:

So what?!!

Grow a pair of yarbles or a backbone. Otherwise, just fuck off. If you don't like SWILL, don't read SWILL -- nobody is forcing you to read this fanzine, are they? Are they? If they are, well then, have them email us and we will happily provide them with more-SWILLish content on demand (for a heafty price -- this would be custom-work after all).

Pith Helmet and Propeller Beanie Tour

The face-to-face participant observation portion of the research
project is starting to wind down a bit(PO will continue via the
internet, etc.). Here are the 2014 tour dates as they currently
stand...

April 2014   Ad Astra 2014 -- Toronto

August 2014   Loncon 3 -- London, UK ???

November 2014 SFContario 5 -- Toronto

SUPPORT SCIENCE FICTION READERS' RIGHTS!   BOYCOTT SFCONTARIO 4!!!

Every year, real science fiction fans are demeaned by a so-called "literary science fiction" convention that panders to those vermin scum -- the self appointed "trufans". These troglodytic living fossils (well, sort of living) shamble about muttering how everybody who is not them is a "fakefan" and not worthy of being permitted to read science fiction. That only they, the "trufen", are legitimate fans and that all the rest of us (a pretty big majority at that) are little more than shithead mundanes masquerading as fans who must be banned from ever attending a fan-run convention or even referring to ourselves as fans. That we should be cast out and damned to trufan hell, aka FanExpoo.

This swinish miniscule niche believe that sf fanzines are of the same, no superior, literary calibre to the works of Clarke, Asimov, LeGuin, Silverberg, Vinge, Egan, MacLeod, Banks, Czernada, Stross, Sawyer, etc. That mediocre scriblings about convention trips, and faan fic, and who the assholes are in the East Wawa SF League, and why nobody under 40 is a trufan, and so on -- are more important than the genre itself. That the genre doesn't matter; only fanzines matter. And only the right type of fanzines matter -- fanzines edited by trufans. These australopithecine intellects claim that they are the ONLY real fans and that the rest of us are mere posers.

Look, it's time to deal with the undead of fandom -- time to purge them from fandom once and for all.

So rise up... It's time to kick over the walkers of these so-called trufen. Direct their scooters into oncoming traffic or down empty elevator shafts. Ream mimeograph stencils up their asses. Force them to guzzle decalitres of corflu. Beat them to a pulp with their own Gestetners, AB Dicks, and Rex Rotarys. Douse them is mimeo ink and set them on fire (but please, not in the hotel -- use the smoking area outdoors). Rid real science fiction fandom of these slothbrained archaic toad-spawn.

The convention concom should be on the side of real SF fans but appear to be in conspiracy with these "trufen". That this convention is a "trufan" plot a ploy to engage in the malicious social persecution of real SF fans. And if the concom wont stand up for real SF fan rights; should they be in favour of perpetuating these "trufen" zombies (complete with rotting flesh scent); well, then they should recieve the same reward.

Stand up for real SF fan rights!!!

      sincerely yours, Ottawa Fandum Ink.

                  the assholes

            printed courtesy of Vile Fen Press

#22   Annual — February 2014

Table of Contents

Front cover art by Rob Murray and Barb Winkler 1975 for Sirius #1; modified by the editor. Back cover photo taken in 1979/1980 by unknown and originally published in Miriad 2; modified by the editor.

SWILL is published quarterly (Spring, Summer, Autumn, and Winter) along with an annual every February - in other words, five times per year.

SWILL

Issue #22 Annual - February 2014

Copyright © 1981 - 2014 VileFen Press

a division of Klatha Entertainment an Uldune Media company

swill.uldunemedia.ca

Editorial: Dumping the Body

James William Neilson

What's it going to be then, eh?

That is the question. As far as I am concerned, as far as SWILL is concerned, traditional "trufan" fandom has already been so thoroughly tolchocked that it is just a bloody, pulpy mass that by all rights should be dead, but persists in croaking out, "But we're the only real fans." Now, I can continue to beat and poke and pummel it more until it loses cellular integrity and is reduced to a goo, but it's getting a bit boring. It's like attempting to have a discussion with a member of the federal Conservative Party -- nothing more than "party-line" parroting and without thought behind it. Same thing, the "trufen" minority will not change, they will not alter their position, they are firm in their belief that they are the one true fandom, and the only ones on the path to fannishness (enlightenment?), and the only ones who can be called science fiction fans. There is no discussion, this lot are like cultists, they have brainwashed themselves.

So be it. It's not worth anybody's time. Most of this lot are ten years older or more than I am, and I am no longer a young malchick myself, so let nature take its course. They are a very small minority anyway and thus, very easy to ignore. And for now, that is what we shall do here at SWILL.

Note: this only applies to the "trufen" minority within traditional fandom, not traditional fandom itself.

So, what axes shall we begin to grind next issue? I am open to suggestions...

In the meantime, what to do with the body??? Shall I use the Fargo wood-chipper, a nice acid bath, or the good old shallow grave with a heavy layer of lime...

Thrashing Trufen: Whose House is This Anyway?

James William Neilson

Taral writes the following in Space Cadet #24:
(http://www.efanzines.com/SpaceCadet/SpaceCadet24.pdf)

"Must we become someone else to belong in our own house?

Oh, but I forget … it isn't our house anymore. We let everyone
in, and now its as much theirs as ours - maybe more so."

To paraphrase my response that appeared in Space Cadet #25 (you
can find that here --
http://www.efanzines.com/SpaceCadet/SpaceCadet25.pdf). No Taral,
you don't have to become a Trekkie, or a member of geek-culture,
etc.; you can just be yourself, a tradfan. Fandom is no longer
the private exclusive hangout of traditional fandom... There is a
tone of regret/self-pity/hoist-by-our-own-petard in the statement
"We let everyone in..." that suggests that tradfandom executed
themselves. This is just rubbish -- with the growth of the
genre, there was no way to keep "them" out. There is no way to
keep fandom the sole property of traditional fandom, other than
bunkering yourselves off from everyone else. Cons like CorFlu
are an example of this -- nobody is going to attend this
convention who isn't a tradfan. So you can bunker yourself off,
in your very own house, but it is going to be a very small or
very empty house.

But what is this "house", after all. Is it fandom? Is it
science fiction? Is it both? I believe for Taral, it is just
fandom and in particular, fandom as it was prior to 1990 (or
possibly prior to 1980). That is all well and fine, but without
being able to teleport yourself back in time to "the good old
days", you cannot turn the clock back, nor can you force your
will upon everyone else; your only alternative is to engage in
self-segregation and exist apart from the rest of the "barbarian"
horde. Kind of like becoming the fannish equivilant of Amish or
Old Order Mennonites. Fine, go ahead, fandom is, essentially, a
democracy, and people can vote with their feet. If you want to
self-segregate, if you want to bunker yourselves away, or live

out on the "trufan" compound, then do so. Just don't snipe back
at the rest of fannish society.

My viewpoint, of course, is very different from that of Taral. I
am not a fan of fandom for fandom's sake. For me, the centre,
is, and always has been, the genre itself. I am a fan of the
genre of science fiction (okay, speculative fiction with a strong
preference for science fiction). Fandom exists only within the
context of the genre itself having existence; thus, the genre is
primary and fandom is a secondary phenomenon. So, from my POV,
if the house belongs to anyone, it belongs to speculative
fiction, not fandom.

LeGuin had a brilliant description of this house -- she wrote
this waaay back in 1974 in the article, "Escape Routes", that was
published in Galaxy magazine and collected in The Language of the
Night (1979). She says:
> "What science, from physics and astronomy to history and
> psychology, has given us the open universe: a cosmos that is
> not a simple, fixed hierarchy, but an immensely complex
> process in time. All the doors stand open, from the
> prehuman past through the incredible present to the terrible
> and hopeful future. All connections are possible. All
> alternatives are thinkable. It is not a comfortable,
> reassuring place. It's a very large house, a very drafty
> house. But it's the house we live in.
>
> And science fiction seems to be the modern literary art
> which is capable of living in that huge and drafty house,
> and feeling at home there, and playing games up and down the
> stairs, from the basement to attic."

That is a really cool, wonderful, enticing, distrubing, and scary
house; and I love it. And it is a house that many creators, from
outside of the print medium, have come to inhabit in increasing
numbers over the past forty years. And not everything produced
has been fantastic (but some of it has been) and often
(unfortunately) it is subpar in comparison to much of the
speculative fiction in the print medium (in particular, in
regards to scientific literacy). And there are many reasons why
that happens[1] and as genre consumers, we often have lower

---

[1] It happens, because the other mediums must be collaborative and content
production is much more expensive. The content for the print medium is
inexpensive to produce, so the individual creator (the writer) remains in near
complete control. That is not going to happen in film and television when the
production costs are going to be in the millions -- there will be decisions

expectations in that regard for film and television SF -- we give an extra suspension of disbelief. But the central point is that there are now many mediums (print, graphic novels, television, film, webseries, podcasts, etc.) all producing speculative fiction content complete with subgenres and subsubgenres. There was a time, back in the mid 1970s when it was possible to read and view all the content produced within the English language for a given year (and even then, there was enough published in print that made this difficult); this is impossible now, even if you are unemployed and all you do is watch and read SF. As has gone the genre, so has the genre's fandom.

Fandom has split into distinct subfandoms, etc. And fandom has changed. Yes, there was indeed a time, in recent memory, about thirty odd years ago, when fandom was still primarilly devoted to the print medium and thus still had a small community feel about it -- not really small, but say a town of twenty thousand. That has disappeared and it is not going to come back. The house has changed, or at least the perception of the analogue for that metaphorical house has changed. Forty years ago, that house would be the size of your average mansion -- a wierd combination of architectual style ranging from the gothic, to surreal, to industrial, to medieval, to futuristic, and so on, with multiple wings leading off the main structure that (like the stairways in Hogwarts) unexpectedly move. Today, it is more akin to a quantum haze that the observer (reader or viewer or both) resolves into some confabulation of strange mansion, theme park, and consumer megaplex. And the only constant, is that the house will continue to change.

Whose house is it? It is speculative fiction's house but, it is also the home of speculative fiction fandom, all of them -- even though their name is not on the deed (a "communal property" sort of common-law arrangement). And on the main floor, in part of the science fiction staging area, at the very, very back by the moulding pulps, is a small, narrow, obscure wing that smells of mimeo ink and old paper inhabited by traditional science fiction fandom -- who try and pretend that the rest of the house doesn't exist.

---

made (rightly or wrongly) that can impact the science, plot, character, the world created, etc. that have more to do with whether or not the money-people think that the average Joe and Jane are going to "get it"; because if they don't "get it", they won't watch it, and there is a hell of a lot more money invested in production than the average $5,000 advance for a novel.

Pissing on a Pile of Old Amazings

...a modest column by Lester Rainsford

Lester goes to cons for the panels. Sure, there are other things to do, like hang around at parties muching on chips and drinking what's to hand, or avoiding filk, or smirking at costumes. But panels are where it's at.

Ninety percent of everything being crap, there need to be rules to get to good panels. Alas, ninety percent of rules are not foolproof either, so Lester recently walked out of a panel that was surely going to become a horror like....here Lester's imagination and recall of horrible scenes fails him....horror like the previous evening's panel when the same person basically trashed it. Horror that would be Lovecraftian if Lester had read a lot of that.

Lester has some pretty simple rules when looking through the programme.

1) The title and description of the panel.

  1a) <u>Criticism in SF</u>--probably ok

  1b) <u>The Infoulence of Academic Criticism in SF</u>--uh oh, DefCon 3 and prepare to escalate as necessary

  1c) <u>Marxist and Feminist Criticism ruinde SF!!</u>--run away, run away!

2) Who is on the panel that Lester recongizes? This cuts both ways. If Lester recognizes the name, it means good or bad, depending.

  2a) Some panelists such as James Nicoll and Karl Schroeder are always interesting. Lester will go to their panels with less regard to the evaluation of 1) above.

  2b) Some panelists like to hear themselves talk; some panelists have strange theories that they insist on propounding, some panelists have to have the first word, the

final word, and all the words in between. Panelsits who have
a been—in their boennet are best avoided.

This is not to say that the rules are sacrosanct, or
disobeying them will be deadly. Lester has seen Charlie
Stross in panels, going way off topic and taking over the
panel. Then again, Charlie Stross doesn't routienly show up
in the sort of local cons Lester frequents. Therefore this
is not a long-term problem.

Lester does ~~withwish~~--and has suggested this--that con goers
~~can~~ should be able to rate panels and/or panelists for the
edification of the ConCom, who after all are too busy to
actually attend a lot of panels themselves. If we can use
the magic of data to get less of what we ~~like~~ don't like,
and more of what we do like, things can only be better, yes?

Lester presumes that his likes and dislikes will be mirrored
by all the other fans who like to go to panels. Hmmm.

A good panel will leave everyone, on both sides of the
table, thinking new thoughts and seeing new points of view.
This is good. ("Science Fiction is a genre of
imagination.!") A bad panel will leave everyone ready to
kick holse in the wall, probably not what the ConCom would
wish. So good panels are better than bad panels! All round!

In conclusion, Lester also want s to thank SFContario for
getting in guests of honour who are actually worth listening
to (at panels, natch), and not just squee-bait celebrities.
It's beneath Lester's dignity to squee, anyway. Now, about
those panel evaluatin sheets....

Flogging a Dead Trekkie:

Violating the ~~Taboos~~ Norms of Science Fiction

Part 6 of 8 — Truly Hard Science

Pre-empted Programming

James William Neilson

Okay, I am taking a single issue break for the SWILL Annual from Malzberg's Taboos of Science Fiction. For those who demand that this action be justified, somehow... Piss off!

But, for those who asked nicely: I am busy writing three stories -- all of which are for anthologies that have deadlines -- that don't fit the Malzbergian norm violations (or if they do/might, were not written as a violation of those norms). I also haven't come up with a good idea yet for a NORM VIOLATION FIVE story.

But, I will in time for the next issue...

Special Feature: Book Reviews

James William Neilson

SWILL hasn't done any book reviews for some time, and I thought
that it was time that there was some. Book reviews were a
regular feature in the original SWILL -- well, sort of... In the
original SWILL the book reviews tended to be either of fictitious
books or of fictitious parodies of real books. With one single
exception, the infamous review of The Probability Broach. Since
the revival of SWILL there has been only one book review, Classic
Butchery, which ripped apart the Baen sequels to The Witches of
Karres. So, here is an experimental trial of real reviews of
real books - this may be a new regular feature/column in future
SWILL annuals.

Over the past twelve months, I have read a fair bit of new
Canadian specfic (and all of it fantasy, believe it or not) among
other things (I'm still playing catch up on MacLeod and Hamilton
and others...). Now, I will state that I don't normally read
fantasy works - too many LoR rip-offs in the 1980s have soured
the well in that regard. So, that means that I usually only read
a fantasy novel after it has been out a few years and everyone is
still talking about how good it is. So, it is a bit of a rare
event (like a SWILL book review column devoted to real books)
that I read fantasy novels within two years of the publication
date, and even more rare when two of them I have read within
months of their release.

Night's Edge: A Turn of Light
Julie E. Czerneda
DAW   896 pgs.   ISBN 978-0756407070

I tend to like Czerneda's work, not all, but most of it. I
really liked In the Company of Others, loved the Species
Imperative trilogy, and enjoyed the Trade Pact trilogy (but not
enough to try the Stratification trilogy). So, a solid enough

9

track record to encourage me to consider embarking on the reading of a Peter F. Hamilton length (almost 900 pages) fantasy novel -- Czerneda's first novel in the fantasy genre. I do this with some trepidation, though. I actually know Julie as an acquaintance and I had also won a copy of this novel in a contest. Thus, I knew that there would come a time when I would have to review the book somewhere, or at least send Julie an email on the subject.

Now, reading this novel did not get off to a smooth start; I hadn't realise how spoiled I had become as a Kobo (like a Kindle for American readers) user over the past four years -- I am rarely an early adopter of new technology, but I bought my Kobo Original within the first week that it came on the market. I found the act of reading a large, trade paperback book to be a tad daunting and so the poor tome languished on my bedside shelf for a couple of months before I finally decided, this is not going to happen, and purchased the Kobo epub of the novel.

Once I actually started the novel, I was captured within the first chapter and drawn into this world. In brief, this is a bildungsroman or coming-of-age tale, centred around the protagonist Jenn Nalynn and the village of Marrowdell. The novel has been described as a romantic fantasy, which in part is a misnomer, at least for me; there certainly is romance, but there is a great deal more as well. The general pace of this novel begins at a quiet and slow pace, like a lazy summer afternoon walk in the country, as you soak up all the local colour -- of which there is an abundance -- before it quickens. Brilliantly, nothing seems forced, everything happens within a strong internal logic and context of the created world. The novel is strongly plotted and engrossing; it fills you and pulls you along with it.

All of the characters are very well developed in the novel, even the very minor characters, and it is difficult for me to pick any favourites. I will confess that, at first, I didn't care too much for the protagonist Jenn Nalynn (though that has more to do with Czerneda's skill in accurately creating an 18 year old character), but over time, Jenn did win me over. Again, all of the characters in the novel are, well people, and by possessing this level of depth, they aid in the construction of making this fictional world appear real.

As this is a fantasy novel, it does involve magic. I really like the magic as depicted in the novel. Marrowdell, and this is as far as I am willing to venture down the path towards spoilers, is by its very location a site of natural magic. The natural magic

that infuses the village is not, in my view, well defined -- it
kind of works with the natural flow of things -- and that is
perhaps the greatest strength of the magic of Marrowdell. We are
made aware of other types of magic, common outside of Marrowdell
such as folk magic and ritual magic, both of which either don't
work within Marrowdell or do work with unexpected and unforeseen
and potential dire consequences. I like the way that magic has
been done in this novel because it has a level of realism built
into it while still remaining ambiguous and situational.

I said earlier that I didn't have a favourite character in the
novel, and that is true in the regular use of the word. I would
say that my favourite character in the novel is the world that it
takes place in. Czerneda has created a world that is wide, old,
and real. Even though the setting is the village of Marrowdell
in the remote north of Rhoth, we get a strong impression of what
exists beyond the borders of the village. Not enough that we can
say that we know Rhoth, or the neighbouring realms of Ansnor and
Elad, or even the capital city of Rhoth, but we can say that we
know of them. We also know of some of the politics, the court
intrigue, the technology, bits of culture, and history of this
world that Marrowdell is located within. There is no sense that
this world is simply a set or backdrop; no, this is a living,
breathing world filled with good and bad, justice and injustice,
and so on. It is a lived in world and a very well constructed
world.

So, to sum up, this is a well written, well plotted novel with
very strongly developed characters, world, and system of magic.
Yes, it is more pastoral that action-packed (but that doesn't
mean that it is devoid of action, but there is no action simple
for action's sake). Yes, it is a romantic fantasy rather than a
heroic fantasy (and yet there are heroic acts and sacrifices).
But it is also, in my mind, a unique fantasy novel and an
excellent one; it is definitely worth the read.

What, no negative comments?!! How can this be a SWILL review?
Well, here we go, though this has to do with a reoccurring theme
in Czerneda's work... Hair! Maybe it's just me, maybe it's
because I'm a guy, I don't know... It is a minor irritant the
amount of time Czerneda spends talking about hair, in particular
the hair of her protagonists. At least Jenn didn't have semi-
sentient hair that was almost a prehensile appendage as does Sira
in the Trade Pact trilogy. There, negative comment made.

Wolf at the End of the World

Douglas Smith
Lucky Bat Books   352 pgs.   ISBN 978-0991800735

Doug Smith is an excellent short fiction writer. I may not like
all of his stories, but I like the majority of his work and he is
a writer who can, apparently, transfer without effort across the
boundaries between fantasy, and horror, and science fiction.
Smith has written a novelette "Spirit Dance" (collected in
Imposibilia) that is takes place prior to the events of Wolf at
the End of the World and involves some of the major characters in
the novel. I have not read this novelette. I thought of doing
so before reading Wolf, but decided against it; I wanted to come
to this novel as fresh as possible for someone already familiar
with Smith's work.

Wolf is Smith's first novel and it is a strong first novel. This
is an urban fantasy and also a coming-of-age story (in part) and
thriller. Smith has drawn upon First Nations myth and legend (in
particular Ojibwe and Cree) for his novel centred around the
Heroka -- shaper-shifters linked to a totem animal (e.g. a wolf)
-- and the black operations division of CSIS (the Tainchel) that
hunts the Heroka. Added into the plot are contemporary issues of
First Nations policy and treatment as well as strong
environmental themes, plus, more First Nations myth in the form
of the Wendigo and the Trickster figure Wsakejack.

What Smith has done well is to make use of First Nations
mythology in, what I believe (wearing my anthropologist hat), is
both an honest and respectful manner. He is not engaged in the
usual cultural-appropriation rip-off that other authors have
done. He has also intentionally made it a point, as a Canadian
of European descent, to be very aware of this issue. His
depiction of Ojibwe culture, modern lifestyle, and beliefs is as
true is possible for an outsider to paint. This is one of the
strong points of the novel.

Both the characters and the world created in Wolf are strong and
believable; Smith has done an admirable job here. However, on
reflection, they lack the same level of depth that exists in
Czerneda's A Turn of Light. I say, upon reflection, as the pace
of Wolf is far more rapid than that of Turn; you don't notice it
during the course of reading, only after the fact. That said,
the story-telling is superbly crafted, strongly plotted, with
good twists, that pulls you along with ease -- definitely a
"page-turner".

My negative comments are slight, this is a first novel -- a
strong first novel -- but still a first novel. While, I would
like to see more of this world, I would also like to see Smith
try his hand with something different before he returns to write
another Heroka novel. My other criticism is that Wolf seems at
times to attempt to play hagazussa in that it appears to be
trying to cross-over the boundary into Young Adult while still
remaining Adult. If indeed this was a goal, it didn't work for
me.

Nevertheless, this is a book to read and I look forward to
Smith's next novel...

Nukekubi
Stephen B. Pearl
Dark Dragon Publishing   254 pgs.   ISBN-10 0986763365

Sigh. I have known Stephen Pearl for over twenty years. Over
those years I have read his fiction, I have not liked it, I have
been polite, I have offered suggestions, and so on...

When I read the reviews of Nukekubi, I thought that maybe he had
begun to develop and decided to give the novel a try. You win
some, you lose some...

In a rather un-SWILL-like fashion; I defer to the words of
Thumper's father; "If you don't have anything nice to say, don't
say anything at all".

Scribbling on the Bog Wall
Letters of Comment

James William Neilson

As I write this, there is one LoC from the usual suspect (Lloyd) and an uber-long LoC from Taral. My comments are, of course, in glorious **pudmonkey**.

1706-24 Eva Rd.
Etobicoke, ON
M9C 2B2

February 11, 2014

Dear James:

Many thanks for another Swill, issue 21, and it's time to see what you and Lester are kvetching about now. Given it's fandom, there's lots to kvetch about.

Fortunately, otherwise what would we kvetch about...

Ideas like FTL travel and transporters and ansibles are great, but are science fantasy. More than anything else, they are plot devices to move the action along to where you want it to be. At one point, SF readers liked the newness of these ideas, but the ideas aren't new any more. We need new plot devices, or if you can't accept the old ideas, it may be time to find another genre of literature to read that has plot devices you haven't seen before. Who knows, maybe SF is obsolete, like Lester says in his column.

SF may or may not be obsolete, just yet. However, there is the risk that this will happen in one way or another in the very near future. One could say that this process is already in progress as

the present and future becomes more and more science-fictional and most of science fiction become indistinguishable from "mainstream" fiction; leaving only obsolete artifacts like space opera, military SF, etc. behind to populate the genre...

Dave Kyle is probably now our most elderly elder statesman when it comes to SF, given that great writers like Fred Pohl have now passed away, and the SF field seems to me to be full of relatively unfamiliar names. I did get a chance to talk to him, wonderful old ideas, but I got the feeling he was perhaps being his age...his memory is affected, and he asked me the same questions about six or seven times within a half hour.

As an elder statesman, Dave is, well elder. Yes, he did wander and repeat himself a bit in conversation with me as well. That is why, I never did get his version of what the Futurians said to him when they found out wrote wrote and printed the "yellow pamphlet". <shrug> Dave was older than I am now when SWILL was first published 33 years ago -- I will cut him some slack and not tolchock him, but I would still like to hear the story (his version)...

The boycott flyer that you circulated at SFContario 4 may just show that fandom is generally humour-impaired. So much of fandom was at one time mostly concerned about fun and a few pranks, but now, we're too serious. I am kinda feeling my age, and seeing that SF and fandom have changed so much as to have left me behind. I could kvetch about that, but I do remember when I got into fandom finding older fans who didn't like me being there, and told me so, but I stuck around. Now, I am one of the older fans, and while I may not have much in common with newer fans, I am determined to not say they shouldn't be there.

Both of us are now, older fans... At times this is scary and at other times, just the way things are. Fannish pranks serious and frivolous do go back to the days of First Fandom and i

remember them in my youth as well. While some of the
SFContario 4 ConCom were upset about the boycott flyer,
others on the ConCom were not and took it as the humour
intended. So, not everyone is humour-impaired; thank the
Gods...

Why haven't aliens visited us yet? Yes, they are more advanced
than we are, but I suspect they are also smarter, too smart to
deal with the likes of us. I suspect once our planet is destroyed
one way or another, the local extraterrestrials will breath a
sigh of relief, and will go about their usual galactic business
with us out of the way.

Oh, so pessimistic... Yes, we may destroy ourselves and we (or
our elites) appear to have selected this as our primary stategy
(because it allows for our elites to continue to maximise profits
and because they honestly believe that they will somehow
survive the immpending doom that they create). As lots and lots
of money can buy you lots and lots of power and resources, it
may be only the majority of humanity that is wiped out and our
elites will carry on.

As for aliens, who knows for certain? Their strategy or planning
or policy could be, very alien. They are probably more
advanced, but probably not too much more advanced (otherwise,
we would have already been colonised, their pressence would
have been detected, etc.). The gamma-ray burst phase transition
hypothesis (that gamma-ray bursts have slowed to a rate that it
now permits complex multi-cellular life to evolve and
potentially develop high technology before another sterilising
burst occurs) would explain our present observations. It could

16

also mean that we are at present, the most advanced technologically.

Of course, it could also be that advanced Type I cilivisations do not attempt to explore and/or colonise the galaxy, that the cost bennefit ratio stops this from occurring (though I don't actually buy that argument, in its entirety, though I do in part -- space travel is hard, difficult, and expensive, interstellar space travel even more so...)

I suspect Yvonne and I will be at Ad Astra for only the Saturday. I also suspect the registration team has been setting aside memberships for us, and know they would be into trouble if that was ever revealed. Nonetheless, we will be there Saturday only, no matter what the badge says. We can't afford hotels any more. I know Ad Astra has had to change hotels and move from Markham to Richmond Hill, but we asked for information on being a dealer at the con, and have received no information, so we have decided to just attend. There are better shows for us to be a dealer at.

Ah, good old Ad Astra. I do not know all of the details with the Ad Astra ConComs, but I do know one thing -- disorganisation is king when it comes to this convention. As for their Dealers' Room, they have fucked things up three years in a row for my old droog, and one year their screw-ups cost him a lot in money (he is NOT attending or having a table this year), so you are probably dodging a bullet there... I have only had to contend with double booking for panels, and stuff like that -- a mild annoyance, only. I have yet to hear back regarding panel suggestions, etc. and I probably won't know for certain anything until Friday of the con when I arrive. If I am on no panels, so be it; I've already paid full membership anyway. So, I will see you both on the Saturday...

Oh, yes, Swill is just so nasty, and is the stick up the arse fandom often needs, so keep going with it. I'll keep responding, but as long as others think, that may be the only other response you'll get. See you next time.

      Yours, Lloyd Penney.

Actually, I don't think SWILL is nasty enough (and neither does Lester) but I haven't hit upon the burning issue to unleash full SWILLness upon (except for Taral, but that IS kind of akin to senior-abuse; definitely droogish, though not entirely SWILLish). SWILL prefers victims that can actually fight back.

However, for nastiness, do read on... Well not the next bit, the bit after that.

SWILL 20 -- I forgot to inlcude this brief exchange with one of my old droogs, Adam, via Facebook.

Adam Smith Yay!! I'm a "known reprobate"!!
1 December 2013 at 17:30

Swill VileFen Press Indeed you were...probably still are in the eyes of that crowd
1 December 2013 at 17:33

Adam Smith Quite likely!
1 December 2013 at 17:42

In SWILL 21, I mentioned that Lloyd told me at SFContario 4 that Taral had a missive for me. Supposedly Taral sent this, but I never received it. His response to SWILL 21 was to resend it with the request that I not make any comments on the piece in-text. <Shrug> Yeah, well, okay. In my opinion, this is not good form, but what the fuck, I will comply...

Loc on Swill 20, *26 Nov 2013*

(I don't really expect this to be published, but under the circumstances, if you intend to, it would be best published in entirely, rather than just cherry-picking points you want to refute. Let me be judged by everything I have to say, or not at all.)

I really think that far too much is being written about the nature or definition of fandom and not enough is being written that you might call "fannish." That is, you, Arnie Katz, Graeme Cameron and even myself have been guilty of late of trying to describe something without borders or exclusive character, for purposes that are impossible to fulfill. I would much rather read what fans are doing than what they should be doing.

At this point, I'm just about worn out on the topic. I've written to Arnie about the same issue of *FanStuff* that you wrote about. I've written to Graeme about his "rant" in the most recent issue of *Space Cadet*. And finally I wrote to Andrew Hooper and his reaction to all this fuss about fandom in *Flag 10*.

Rather than write all the same old stuff about the same old subject one more time, let me just quote myself from my letter to Arnie's *FanStuff*:

Graeme and I have discussed his various projects to infuse new life into fanzine fandom for several months ... if not years. He can't be faulted for enthusiasm or for lack of ideas. Just as I can't be faulted for not being overly optimistic about his chances of

success. The Canadian fanzine archive he began -
http://www.cdnsfzinearchive.org/ - is only the latest project.
While he's made a good start, it's hard to predict how extensive his
reach will be. To live up to Graeme's goals, it won't be enough to
store a mere smattering of *DNQs*, a few *Monthly Monthlies*, a handful
of *Lights*, the *Energumens* and *Amors* that I scanned a few years ago,
and a glut of recent zines published only in the last few years.
But can Graeme find a significant source of *Queebshots, A Bas,
Macabres, CanFans, OSFic Quarterlies, Orcas, Simulacrums, Winding
Numbers, Brazzors, Thangorodrims, Pantekhnicons* and all the dozens
of other Canadian fanzines that made at least some ripple in the
ocean of fanzines in their day?

There is the question, too, of whether such an archive serves fandom
best by specializing. It's your opinion that an archive serves
fandom best by ignoring national boundaries. On the other hand, it
is Graeme's particular interest to compile Canadian fanzines … and
it does no harm. Who, after all, is fully knowledgeable about all
of fanzine fandom? In my own writing about fanhistory I've mainly
focused on Canadian fandom because it was what I knew about … and
who else would write about it? Everyone else is busy immortalizing
their particular corner of the fannish universe.

Will Graeme's archive bring any new fanzine fans to the fold? I
doubt it, and have said so forcefully on several occasions. But
Graeme claims that his site enjoys a large number of hits -
certainly more than my defunct blog ever did, or it might not be
defunct. What neither of us can answer, though, is whether people
searching for fanzines are looking for *ours* … or looking for
fanzines about pop music, breeding goldfish, collectible antiques,
modern poetry or model railroading … and likely going away
disappointed. So far, Graeme hasn't discovered a single newbie for
fanzine fandom out of all those hundreds of hits. I don't find that
encouraging.

But *Graeme* is ever hopeful.

There is also Graeme's Canadian annual fanzine achievement award.
This has been problematical from the start. There are so few
Canadian fanzine fans that there is a real danger of giving the
awards to the same half-dozen or so people every year. The first
two year's were selected by Graeme himself, and were as predictable
as you might expect. With one or two eccentric choices of Graeme's,
it was the same the year after. There was an actual ballot this,
the third year, but, for the most part, the names were still

familiar. I'm not sure what can be done about it. In Canadian fandom there are only two clubzines and three faneditors such as myself who anyone outside of some tiny enclave is likely to ever know about. (And our fandom is *itself* a tiny enclave!) There is only one fanartist, three fanwriters and two letter hacks. Another three of four Canadian fans attend Corflu when they can … for what that's worth.

But *Graeme* is ever hopeful.

It all started, of course, with his massive encyclopedia of Canadian fandom, online at http://canadianfancyclopedia.shawwebspace.ca/. Although incomplete and likely never to be finished, it is a treasure trove of information about Canadian fandom that I suspect is sadly underutilized.

Graeme's latest attempt to revitalize fanzine fandom lies in his regular fan column at Amazing Stories, http://amazingstoriesmag.com/. To present date, they've run 8 or 9 or Graeme's articles, and I have to admit they have been brisk and entertaining. They would look good in any fanzine … for that matter, they might raise the quality of Graeme's own fanzines, if he'd care to dwell on the irony of doing his best writing for someone else. Also writing for the "club house" section of Amazing stories are Steve Fahnestalk and Earl Kemp. Graeme has even suborned me into lending a hand, though so far my involvement has been limited to a single, as yet unpublished cartoon for one of his upcoming columns.

Surprisingly, the "club house" columns at Amazing Stories might just reach receptive souls among the readers. I don't have great expectations, mind you. Just because a fan reads science fiction, and reads *about* science fiction, it doesn't follow that he wants to write about it, or - even less likely - write about the subculture that formed around science fiction. But I think the columns at Amazing Stories have a better chance of finding fresh blood for fanzine fandom than any other plan I've heard lately.

And Graeme, for once, may have reason to be hopeful.

Now from my letter to Graeme's Space Cadet 23:

  To begin with, when I try to argue with someone wearing two
  different hats, I have trouble knowing who I'm arguing with. Is it

Graeme the scold, putting Old School fans in their place for not opening their homes and hearts to 15-year-old zombie enthusiasts? Or is it Graeme the sage, who is philosophical about the graying and gradual extinction of the fandom he knew and loved?

No matter. I intend to talk entirely about myself and my point of view, anyway.

From my perspective, fandom was a fairly welcoming place in the past … up to a point. All you had to do to be welcome was show an interest in science fiction - which was just about entirely the printed word in those days - and to mind your manners. Demanding a place of honour the moment you set foot in a club, or insisting that everyone adopt your revolutionary new spelling reform, would get you labeled as a geek, of course. Even geeks got over it sometimes, though, so if eventually the rough edges of your personality wore smooth, you would finally fit in. Up to a point. There were still personal cliques that, for one reason or another, you would never be at home in - and if you were sensible, you realized this and had *no desire* to force your way in. It was easy to imagine that closed circles were elites, and that you were barred because you weren't one of the Beautiful People, but, in fact, it was more likely because you didn't play poker or couldn't talk publishing shop. Easy to mislead yourself about this, mind you. I tended to.

However, fandom today isn't what it was in 1975. Throwing the door open to all-comers won't necessarily bring in people who want to talk Cordwainer Smith or Theodore Sturgeon with you. It's more apt to bring in people who want to talk about *Game of Thrones* or *Buffy the Vampire Slayer*. When that happens, what do you do? Smile, try to make some inane comments in reply, and watch helplessly as your home fills up with more and more strangers, who haven't the slightest interest in your reading or your hobby?

That's the predicament I see Old School fandom in. It isn't that older fans are unfriendly, or that we believe there's something inferior about people with an interest in Japanese animation or the SCA. Hardly that. But it isn't *our* interest. Attracting such people isn't why we hold open house. If it was, where *do* we draw the line? Martial arts? Viniculture? Go-Kart racing? Fandom can't be for *everyone* … or it isn't *anything!*

It would be just a format for doing whatever you like. Now, *oddly enough*, that is exactly what I've been arguing lately: that as fandom disseminates into the mainstream, it has ceased to be about anything in particular, and is increasingly just *a way of doing things.*

For years, this development has been hidden by the fact that most fans actually *do* have more interests than just reading science fiction. Most will *watch* it, either on TV or the Big Screen. Some also enjoy costuming, gaming, arts & crafts, comics and what-have-you. Collecting other kinds of genre-fiction is also common. So, despite the influx of people into fandom over the last two or three decades, many of whom have had little interest in books that aren't about *Dr. Who* or the starship *Enterprise*, it has been easy for Old School fans to accommodate them. Up to a point.

At some point, however, the newbies began to outnumber the establishment. More to the point, as they demanded more and more attention paid to their particular interests, there has been greater and greater reluctance to cater to a minority interest - which is what Old School fandom is becoming. The very nature of fandom, its purpose and identity, has become the stakes between two conflicting views. Was it a fandom about science fiction, primarily the written word …or fans of the written word just a modest splinter group among many groups that make up popular "geek" culture?

In other words, is the hit TV show, *Big Bang Theory*, the model for modern fandom?

None of this really has much to do with me, however. You see, my dirty little secret is that I'm *not* a science fiction fan. Not in the classic sense of reading it every day, caring deeply about what happens in the SF sub-culture or feeling any urge to proselytize it to the uninitiated. SF is everywhere. Everyone who is under the age of 35 and speaks English (or French, in Quebec) is saturated with science fiction images and ideas, whether they read SF or not. SF is able to look out after itself without my zealotry.

What I've had to face up to is that I'm a hobbyist. I like to draw, write and self-publish. It happens that my background is science fiction fandom of the Old School, so that is my natural idiom. I frankly don't know what I'd do without it. Still, I wouldn't care if the last Arthur C. Clarke novel was burned in a bonfire, if *Analog* went bankrupt or if the Scientologists bought a life-time achievement Hugo for L. Ron Hubbard. Okay … I'd care about *that* … but only because it would be in such deplorable taste, not because it would hurt science fiction. As far as making it more acceptable to the general public, it might even *help*.

Anyone who is interested in my hobby - fanzine publishing - is
perfectly welcome to take the same pleasure in it that I do. It's
just unfortunate that few do. Gawd knows, I've tried to use new
information technologies to reach new readers … but I've only had
limited success. The fact is that few people find printed material
very exciting - most printed matter that the average person is
exposed to is crumpled up in a ball as soon as it is extracted from
the mail box, and immediately thrown in the recycle bin. What's
exciting about *that?* Especially when, for only $319.95, you can have
a pair of interactive sunglasses that connect to the internet, let
you leave voice mail, plan a vacation in Disney World, download the
present location of everyone you know and score a fix - all while
live-streaming your wait in line for a latté at Starbucks. Maybe
the only reason *I* don't have the iCrap to do all that is that I
can't afford it.

I do what I can. I publish digitally, and email to my readers. I
keep up a lively presence on a couple of artists' sites and on
FaceBooger. Probably a third of my readers are people I've reached
out to who are *not* members of conventional fandom. My blog was a
failure, never gaining more than 11 regular readers, as far as I
could tell. But I'm not alone - Brad Foster seems to have abandoned
his as well. I'm not altogether unhappy with the situation as it
is. The other side of the coin is obvious, however. Millions of
readers *could* download my fanzines, write to me, talk about me all
over the internet, or - more creatively - become involved in my
hobby by publishing their own fanzines. Clearly, however, millions
of people *don't.* I've tried to deliver the message … we've tried …
fanzine fandom has tried … but it's just not being received. This
is why I think no amount of welcoming newcomers will work. They're.
Just. Not. Interested.

It's worth saying again. They're just not interested.

What more can we do? Put on a steampunk outfit, learn Klingon and
chatter about *Elfquest* incessantly … and *deny who we are?* Must we
become someone else to belong in our own house?

Oh, but I forget … it isn't our house anymore. We let everyone in,
and now its as much theirs as ours - maybe more so. And I nearly
forgot … at best, I'm only a casual science fiction fan, so it's no
concern of mine. I just publish fanzines about myself and, at
present, I think that's the best possible thing I can be doing.

Finally, this succinct little squib from my loc to Andy's Flag:

I feel as though I have been writing entirely too much about fandom lately ... why, I just wrote to Graeme Cameron's *Space Cadet*, expressing my thorough disinterest in spreading the fannish gospel to the fans of tomorrow. Seeing how they don't seem interested, it appears to be a waste of time. We old folk can adapt all we want to the new digital media, but they aren't going to adapt to us by one single pixel: so we can become them or we can remain ourselves. I opt for remaining myself.

I wish I had thought of saying just that to Graeme ... it would have saved me more than two entire pages of typing.

It is, I think, the happiest distillation ever of my thoughts on the recent development of fandom. Had I been able to say it this way a few years ago, I would have saved myself far more than merely *two pages* of writing...

***

You were somewhat off base in your description of OSFiC, I think. You saw a single cross section of it at a particular time, and have characterized the entire club throughout its 17-or-18 year life as it appeared to you from one, brief encounter. Suppose instead of a science fiction club, OSFiC had been a tribe of native Indians in Brazil that you met on a canoe trip up the Amazon. Would you feel justified in describing their society as one that wore blue jeans, spoke Spanish as a second language and practiced a form of nativistic religion heavily influenced by Roman Catholicism just because that was how you saw them in 1976? Or would you be more likely to be aware that their lifestyle had probably changed many times over the centuries? Granted, a science fiction club rarely lasts more than a decade or two, but the era of OSFiC you were familiar with covered a short period of time in which the club was run by a handful of people who you didn't know well. You likely knew much less about the club before that time, and fairly little about OSFiC's latter years. There were about four quite distinct phases in its short history.

It's unlikely you knew much about the less prominent cliques in OSFiC either. But though they didn't fill the club's newsletter or plan the meetings, they had their own foibles and pursued their own purposes.

You are also completely inaccurate in your remark about the club's harassment of fans with professional or semi-professional ambitions. Among the in-group were Robert Charles Wilson, arguably the best science fiction writer in Canada. As was Patrick Nielsen Hayden, one of the editors at Tor Books. Barry Kent Mackay was a noted columnist in The Star and a well-known naturalist painter. Jim Allan had a book published on Tolkien languages. Although it was a few years later, and a different clique, Robert J. Sawyer was program director of OSFiC for a time. Phyllis Gotlieb was a personal friend of mine and honorary member of the club. I think John Robert Colombo might have been an honourary member as well … as have been other noted writers like Donald Kingsbury and Karl Schroeder. This is what I mean by saying you didn't know OSFiC well enough to intelligently comment on it.

And do you really think it necessary to descend to the level of calling people "sloth-brained" and "assholes."[2] There's a time and a place for such passionate language, but surely not in a piece of writing that is pretending to be impartial … even scholastic. Frankly, Neil, coming from a sociologist, I find it unprofessional.

Number one, despite what you may believe; SWILL does not cherry-pick our LoCs. If it is a LoC, we print the whole damn thing and insert my commentary as the LoC goes along. Only social media "LoC's or reviews in other zines are edited, as they were not written as an actual letter.

As to your LoC to Fanstuff #41, my response in part will appear in Fanstuff #42 -- which I had expected to be out before SWILL

---

[2] Second last paragraph, page 8 of Swill 20. "Our only point of difference is that I think that the traditional fen of Toronto have taken exclusivity and assholery to the level of a high art form. Though, that could just be because they are Torontonians, who view Toronto as the centre of the universe … "

Page 22, first paragraph. "Then, they either launch into nostalgia about the "good, old days" or into diatribe about how this subcultural trait is lost on the sloth-brained "fakefans" (everyone who is not them) of today."

#20 -- and the first two thirds of the Editorial on SWILL #20 is what was sent to Fanstuff.

As to your LoC to Space Cadet #23, I had my own comments regarding that issue and both of our LoCs appeared in Space Cadet #24 and my responses to your LoC can been found in Space Cadet #25 (http://www.efanzines.com/SpaceCadet/). In addition, it is dealt with in "Whose House is This Anyway?" within this issue.

In regards to your LoC to Flag #10, I have only one comment. Nobody is going to adapt to your version of traditional fandom, because nobody (okay, hardly anyone) is going to choose to live as if it was 1984 in 2014. Especially if they were born after 1984. Yes, as I have said before, do be yourself; just don't be all "superior-than-thou-looking-down-your-nose" at the rest of fandom.

As for your commentary that appears below the

***

I will attend to some of that here and the rest within the Endnote.

Regarding OSFiC, which I know that you were heavily involved in. It was not just "one, brief encounter". I used to go down to Toronto three to four times a year to attend OSFiC meetings in

1975 and 1976 (I was in the UK for 1977 and the first half of 1978) and when I moved to Toronto in mid-1978, I was regularly attending OSFic meetings for a while. I quickly tired of it because, I did not find it a welcoming environment and even though I was now living in the city, I was still treated as if I did not. As I have recounted in SWILL and Space Cadet, I began to hang out more with people my own age, some of whom I met via OSFiC. In my crowd, there were a couple of people who continued to attend OSFiC meetings and reported back on what news there was. Most of us found what was going on was irrelevant. And to ourselves and our interests within fandom as we saw it, it was. Who the fuck cared about some fan feud that happened back in 1970 and shit like that? We were interested in what was happening in the genre?

So, no: I am not basing my view of OSFiC from a single teen-age encounter. It is based upon multiple encounters from my teens to my early twenties and not just my views, but the combined views of others plus my own. Were any of the people in my crowd members of the prominent or less prominent cliques within OSFiC between 1976 and 1982; no, I do not think that they were. Whatever view we had was a "laity-eye" view of the organisation at best and never that of the "clergy", like yourself. It is the view from those outside of the inner circle and outside of the circle period as well of that organisation -- it is no less a valid POV than that of thsoe within the inner circle (incomplete albeit, but nevertheless, valid).

Okay, you are very, very defensive of OSFiC. You missed part of the context in the article -- true I do not cue the reader in this short piece, which maybe I should have. Paragraph One introduces the concept of the term exchange culture, with some digs at traditional fandom, while speaking in the general. Paragraph Two is also speaking in the general, but offers the specifics of observations of the exchange culture as it was practiced within OSFiC in the mid-late 1970s. Paragraph Three is general and not specific (i.e. not about OSFiC) -- it is tarring tradfandom in general for this behaviour that was taking place in fandom at that time period, because the writers were all bitching about it -- in particular Ellison. Paragraph Four links the exchange culture as portrayed in Paragraph Two to fanzine fandom and states that the decline in fanzine fandom has resulted in a decline in the exchange culture.

My questions are, as someone who was not really a part of the exchange culture in traditional fandom, was my depiction in Paragraph Two mostly correct or mostly in error? Do you agree with the statements in Paragraph Four of how there is a strong connexion between the exchange culture and publishing print (on paper not pdf) fanzines? Do you not? With the near absence of print fanzines today, do you think that this has had an impact on the exchange culture within traditional fandom? Or an I in error for making this connexion?

As for making up the word, "assholery" to describe the exclusive attitude of tradfandom in the mid-1970s -- this is aimed at OSFiC but also at the rest of traditional fandom from that time period. Note, that I do offer a potential excuse, that this was not a traditional fandom attitude, but just a Torontonian attitude (even though I personally think that the exclusive attitude was indeed a traditional fandom attitude that was compounded and amplified by being Torontonians).

As for the use of the word "sloth-brained"; FYI, that was not directed at OSFiC or traditional fandom, but how traditional fandom, in general, views anyone who is not a traditional fan. Either as some poor sod who has suffered brain damage and is to be looked down upon or avoided, or as an ignorant fool who just has to be placed upon the right path and/or villified should they decline the "assistance".

As for the rest; read onward to the Endnote...

Endnote: A Boot-to-the-Head

James William Neilson

The Editor (Evil Arch-Anti-Fan) has been Charged by the "Saintly" Advocate of Traditional Fandom (Taral Trufan) with Committing Behaviour Unbecoming an Academic - therefore a crime against society, an act of unprofessionalism, and bias.

In response to these charges I state most definitely that I use words like "sloth-brained", "toad-spawn", "assholery", "fuck", and other not nice and sometimes negative and off colour made-up words in SWILL. Is this behaviour unbecoming of an academic, an act of unprofessionalism, or evidence of bias - within the context of a textbook, an academic paper, or an article in a peer-reviewed journal - it would be, but this is not a peer-reviewed journal, a paper presented at an academic conference, or a textbook, is it? This is SWILL, after all, and SWILL is not an academic work for an academic audience, it is an amateur magazine, a fanzine. It may not be the kind of fanzine Taral is used to or likes or even wants to consider as being a fanzine; but, at the end of the day, it is a fanzine. Or as Graeme wrote of the original SWILL in the Canadian Fancyclopedia years ago and before the current revival; SWILL is "A perzine... What would normally be called a crudzine, but in this case it's not due to lack of ability but rather deliberate policy. Opinionated and rather rude, depending on 'shock' humour. Lots of swearing. Agressive satire."

In other words, SWILL is a fanzine.

And while SWILL may blur the lines between academic journal and a fanzine by using footnotes and occasionally citing sources, that doesn't make it a scholarly journal; not at all.

Look here, Taral, as in the quote from Graeme above, SWILL is a "perzine", a personal fanzine. In other words a fanzine that contains and/or reflects the personal interests of the editor; obviously, one of my personal interests is giving traditional fandom, in particular self-professed "trufans", a boot-to-the-head, or two. Yeah, I am an anthropologist, and a sociologist, and an academic, and a professor, and a fan of science fiction, and (I think just because I pub SWILL) I am marginally a traditional fan, and I am an anti-fan (in regards to self-proclaimed "trufans"), I'm a parent, a middle-aged anarcho-syndicalist, and so on. As the editor of SWILL I juggle my many hats - like Goffmanesque masks and frames - and sometimes a column or editorial is written with one of my academic hats. But that mask does slip or is exchange for another and that nihilistic anti-fan persona is revealed - this is SWILL, after all.

There is a reputation to uphold and all that (as it is, Lester finds the current SWILL too wimpy). Yeah, self-created "trufen" have been SWILL's preferred target since its inception - you may not like that (since you're the one who is being poked with a stick), but that is just tough shit - and the "trufen" tradfans will remain in the gun sight as SWILL's favourite Fritz to tolchock. Just the way things are and that is not going to fucking change.

SWILL may, from time to time, appear quasi-academic, but that is an illusion; for SWILL is simply a cross between an op-ed piece and personal reflection, with a punkish attitude and identity. SWILL, the fanzine, is not academic journal.

Here is an actual sample of academic writing:

> On the other hand, there is the question raised by postmodernists - is there such a thing as definitions and terms that have "universal" or "wide" acceptance? And this is a good point. In Bakker's version of Pierce he presents as the INSOR model - Interpretive Network, Sign (or Sign System), and Operationalised Representation. Interpretive Network is what Pierce called the Interpretant - an interpretive community or

network of individuals who share a common sign system.
The Sign System, or Sign, is the set of symbols - the
code - shared by members of an Interpretive Network.
Operationalised Representation, what Pierce termed as
the Representant, is a semiotic system of
representations that are known by almost all members of
an Interpretive Network. At the end of the day, all of
our knowledge are signs. All of our definitions and
terms are also signs (Bakker, 2005, 2008).

This was written as a paper presented at an academic conference,
so it is a less formal style than that of an academic journal.
Had it actually appeared in a peer-reviewed journal, it would be
even drier (phrases like "on the other hand" and "at the end of
the day" would have been edited out as too colloquial). This
passage is quite readable and senior undergraduates in sociology
or anthropology should be able to read and comprehend its
content. So this is an example of academic writing. What Taral
refers to as being academic gibberish which he would lampoon as
"Opportunalised Reformatation of the Internalive Newark in the
socio-economic technobabble, blah, blah, blah." or something like
that. Well, you can't have it both ways fanboy...

You cannot damn SWILL for not behaving as a peer-reviewed journal
and also rubbish it for the times it appears quasi-academic. And
you cannot tell me, the creator of SWILL what this zine is or
what its tone should be, either. It is not as if the tone of
SWILL is any surprise, right. One would hope not. Frankly,
Taral, you're asking for a right tolchocking, you're asking for a
boot-to-the-head.

Pith Helmet and Propeller Beanie Tour

The face-to-face participant observation portion of the research
project is starting to wind down a bit (PO will continue via the
internet, etc.). They shifted my teaching time for the summer so
Loncon is now a no go. However, I will be attending...

April 2014   Ad Astra 2014 -- Toronto

November 2014   SFContario 5 -- Toronto

CODA

A list of SWILL volumes:

Original SWILL	issues 1 through 7
SWILL 2011	issues 8 through 12
SWILL 2012	issues 13 through 17
SWILL 2013	issues 18 through 22
SWILL 2014	issues 23 through 26
SWILL 2015	issues 27 through 30
SWILL 2016/2017	issues 31 through 35
SWILL Annuals: Volume 1	issues 36 through 40

Vile Fen Press

a division of Klatha Entertainment an Uldune Media company